Dr. Jaerock Lee's Testimonial Memoirs

TASTING
ETERNAL
LIFE
BEFORE
DEATH

I0616584

Dr. Jaerock Lee

URIM
BOOKS

TASTING ETERNAL LIFE BEFORE DEATH by Dr. Jaerock Lee

Published by Urim Books (Rep.: Kyungtae Noh)
73, Yeouidaebang-ro 22-gil, Dongjak-Gu, Seoul, Korea
www.urimbooks.com

Copyright © 2003 by Dr. Jaerock Lee
ISBN : 978-89-7557-245-6 (03230)
Translated by Dr. Kooyoung Chung. Used by permission.

Previously published in Korean by Urim Books, Seoul, Korea.
Copyright © 1987

First Edition 1st Printing March 2003
Second Edition 1st Printing April 2004
2nd Printing August 2005
Third Edition 1st Printing January 2008
Fourth Edition 1st Printing January 2009

Edited by Dr. Geumsun Vin
Designed by Editorial Bureau of Urim Books
Printed by Yewon Printing Company
For more information contact at urimbook@hotmail.com

ACKNOWLEDGMENTS

First of all, I give all thanks and glory to God who has guided me to publish this book.

Lately God urged me to collect the materials of my past life and publish a book. It was a burden to me to write about my passed days, because I was not literarily minded, and because I was not able to spare much time. Thinking back on my past life, however, it has been miraculous all by itself. God healed my seven years of sickness and then called me as His servant. Every single hour up to now, God has accompanied me.

I realized that to publish this book to testify God to non-believers must be pleasing to Him. Although I had made up my mind to do this important job, I was sorry that I did not know where I would start. Here, God selected Senior Deaconess Geumsun Vin as the overall editor. Senior Deaconess Vin collected all the necessary materials, arranged them in appropriate order for publishing, and edited the entire work from the beginning to the end. I thank Senior Deaconess Vin for her devoted endeavor and effort. I believe God may reward her with abundant blessings.

I am glad that this is the first book for us, Manmin Central Church, to publish. I hope this book may play a significant role, not as my own personal introduction, but as a powerful tool that testifies to the love and the grace of Jesus Christ and His miraculous works and providence, guiding the readers to new hope for salvation and eternal life.

I also thank the translator, Deacon Taebong Kwon, and his American friends, Mrs. Kim Clark and Mr. Tyler Dixon, and the staff of Translation Bureau who earnestly helped in editing this English version.

Jaerock Lee

CONTENTS

PART 1: AT THE DOORSTEP OF DEATH • 1

0 You'd better die
0 When I was young
0 The struggle
0 As time passes by

PART 2: THE MIRACLE • 27

0 Affection
0 Sick body and broken heart
0 Immortal wretched life
0 My elder sister
0 My reborn life

PART 3: OH, GOD! • 63

0 My new life
0 Please help me to forgive the others
0 Until the end of my journey

PART 4: CHARACTER PRODUCES HOPE • 91

0 I was a sinner
0 The cross of the Lord
0 The living God
0 If you can?
0 Starting a church
0 The vessel

PART 5: GOD HAS ACCOMPANIED ME • 147

0 The blessed
0 The voice of the Lord
0 The Sovereign
0 The revelation

PART 6: PRECIOUS LIFE • 179

0 Recollection
0 My past
0 My present
0 My future
0 Thanks for everything

PART 7: MY BELOVED ONE • 211

0 All the glory to God
0 By His will
0 Everlasting life in heaven

1
AT THE DOORSTEP OF DEATH

You'd better die

In the early summer, 1972

The season was changing and the fresh green was covering the whole land. The fragrance of the acacia came to me on the breeze and touched my nose with a crisp tickle. It was time for everybody to smell the freshness and vitality of the summer. But my body and my spirit were still in winter like frozen ice. As time passed, thick ice melted into the streams, winter woke up from its long sleep, and new buds appeared to decorate spring. However, my winter had no promise of changing to spring, but only to deep sighs.

As usual, I was lying on the floor under a dirty blanket in my single-room house for the whole day. I saw cotton-like clouds through a partially opened window. Those clouds reminded me of my mother's warm bosom. If I were one of those clouds, I would travel the whole peninsula without any worry and anyone to envy.

'I am just thirty years old, at the age of vitality and fortitude, which is the peak of life. But now I'm looking at my body being destroyed part by part, day by day...'

My tears had dried up, and my hope of being cured was gone. Only one desire, to stay alive, was remaining in me.

I was still looking at the beautiful jade green sky through the window. Intermittently the sun showed its brilliant face to me among the passing clouds. I wanted to feel that warm sunshine on my face and whole body. Leaning against the wall, I was barely able to lift the upper half of my body. I immediately felt extreme pain in my knees and I became anemically dizzy. I had a strong desire to escape my room, so I grabbed the stick that I needed to get to the bathroom. Leaning heavily on it, I opened the door and took my first step outside. Wow! I almost shouted because the fresh air and brilliant sunshine outside were so wonderful.

When I managed to get to the front yard with trembling legs, I broke into a cold sweat. The view of the Han River stretching out before me made me feel peaceful and cool.

I remember the hill of Gumho-dong where I lived. On the hill a lot of blockhouses were huddled close to one another. Most of them were illegally constructed. In my village most of the residents were poor but warm-hearted. When they occasionally saw me, I could read in their eyes the pity they felt for me.

'When the villagers climb the steep hill, I can see the beads of sweat on their faces. They don't complain about the hard climb. They just manage their lives to the best of their ability.'

On that day I could not continue to look at them moving about so vitally. Feeling confused and exhausted, I just wanted to lie down. Leaning on my stick and nearly crawling, I returned to my room.

Mother's lamentation

My room was humid and smelled of my dirty blanket that had never been rolled up, and of the medicine boiling on the stove in the kitchen. My room was the only place for me to take rest and protect myself.

After resting for a while, I heard someone knock on the door. I was wondering who it could be. My wife left for work early in the morning, and my daughters had just left to play with their friends.

"Son, it's me. Are you in?"

Mother? What brought her to Seoul? She's quite elderly at seventy. It must be hard for her to come up the hill.

She came into the room and looked at the messy surroundings and at me, her sick skinny son, and for a while said nothing.

"Hi, Mother. Why don't you sit over here?"

Tears welled up in my mother's eyes and she began to cry uncontrollably. She wept bitterly, beating the floor with her hands.

"You, bad boy! You'd better die. Die now! Do you know how much suffering this is for your wife and children? Do you know how piercing this is to my heart? I'll be happy if you die."

My mother wept for a long time. I could understand she really wanted me to die. I was shocked to know this, although at the same time I understood her. Being shocked and lost, I stared at her blankly.

'Is she too old? How come she wants me to die now? Did she climb up the high hill to say that to me, her son, who has had no nursing for years? Is this my mother? How could she do this?'

I was so sorry that I could not stop shedding tears. How devotedly had she taken care of her husband and children? How willingly had she managed all housing chores in the countryside for her family? She was the mother who searched all of the remedies for me for several years, but now she doesn't want to share my pain any more. I was sad to know this.

Conflicts

Deeply wrinkled face, heavy-weighted shoulders and tiny old body... These features of my mother made me feel sad. I believed my frustration and agony were greater than my mother's.

There were more things that saddened me:

We were living in a monthly rented single-room house, which was an illegally constructed cement-block building. There was only a dresser as furniture, a pile of unfolded blankets, a bowl with some leftover liquid medication, a roughly shaved wooden stick, and a bunch of medicine bags in the corner of my room.

'Sure, why not? To die, I think, would be the best for my family. I don't have to be a burden to them any more. At first they'll be sad, but then they'll forget me, living in a new situation. Yes, I'd better say goodbye to this world as soon as possible.'

I looked at my mother still crying and made up my mind to die. I could not look at my mother any longer. I turned my face toward the window. The warm sunshine beat on my face and glared in my eyes. Right then a craving for life suddenly arose in my heart. My decision to die was immediately changed.

'Surely I'm still young! It is too early for me to die. I cannot finish my life in this miserable state, burdening my family members. I must stay alive so that I may compensate my family for their loss. I don't want them to remember me this way.'

I did not know where I got this strength. From the bottom of my heart a certain hot aspiration for life was arising within me.

'The diseases are destroying all of my body, but I will beat them down eventually.'

Foolish Deaths

Feeling torn between life and death, I tried to look back on my life. I remembered that I had attempted to commit suicide before. At that time I was not as desperate as I am now.

There are people who commit suicide before they know what life is, what death is, and what they have to live for in this world.

Some of them become so frustrated that they kill themselves when they fail to accomplish their life goals. Businessmen commit suicide when they ruin their business. Twelfth grade students choose to die because they fail in the college entrance exams, and some students from elementary, middle and high school also do so because they are so afraid of being scolded by their parents for their bad test results. Some people give up their lives because they cannot accomplish their wills. Through mass media we often hear about these people who kill themselves.

There is another group of people committing suicide in the name of love. Although they say their love rises over national borders and peril of life, they choose to die when they cannot get married or their beloved ones betray them. Even some people die to follow after their loved ones' death. They would consider that love is the only reason for them to live in this world. That is ridiculous. They do not care how precious life is.

Truly worthy life

On the other hand, there is another group of people who

cannot help but die in the hospital. A lot of people, 'hospitalized' by unexpected accidents or fatal diseases, are desperately striving against death.

Some people commit suicide because of their painful lives, on the other hand some people rise from near death with tenacious aspirations for life. However, the number of people dying is much larger. We must know that life is precious. We must appreciate what real life is and what the object of life is. No matter what circumstances we are in, we must cherish life itself. Then we will not cut off our precious lives at random.

I had even attempted to kill myself when I was healthy. However, when I heard from my mother, 'I'll be happy if you die,' a craving for life arose in me like a burning fire.

My mother's wailing pierced my heart and made tears well up in my eyes. As I looked up, trying to keep back my tears, some clouds were floating in the blue sky, as if they would comfort me. Without effort my mind raced back to my cheerful childhood and beautiful hometown. How beautiful it was! How healthy I was! Oh, I miss those days when so many people loved me!

When I was young

My hometown

My hometown is Jangsung, Jullanam-do. This town is famous for its beautiful scenery and clean water. The beautiful scenery of the Noryoung Mountains extends to the hills surrounding Jangsung Town.

Jangsung is known as a place where the classical scholarly manner strongly affects the residents. Many of the residents, young or old, still wear the Korean traditional costume, Hanbok, more often than people of other areas do. They are so conservative that they, living in a town of scholars, emphatically practice the subject of courtesy.

My father was a scholarly man with some heroic airs who was widely knowledgeable in Chinese classics and poems. During the Japanese colonial period he handled trading businesses, traveling between Japan and Korea. Right after Korea was liberated, he quit his business and looked for a place to live in seclusion. He found a good place in Jangsung, so my family moved there from Muan when I was three years old. This is why I think of my hometown as Jangsung.

My family settled into a village where most of the residents had the last name, Chun. Although it was not easy for a different-named family, my father bought some land for farming and built a house to live in that Chun-last-named village.

My father, a scholar of Chinese classics

When I was young, my father was always at home alone and constantly reading. He sometimes had uninvited visitors, though. Whenever his friends came to see him, they enjoyed themselves chanting poems or chatting about classics over the drinking table. I also remember that my father occasionally left home, traveling alone for a long time. Then my mother had to take the responsibility for the family. She had to work hard to raise three sons and three daughters.

I, as the youngest son, was my parents' favorite. When I was five years old, my father taught me the 1,000 basic Chinese characters. He used to talk to me about famous historic stories. This made me dream of a lot of things. To be a great man was one of my dreams. After I entered elementary school, he took me to the place where the candidates, running for (provincial or national) lawmakers and president, made speeches. Since then I started to cultivate my dream to be a parliamentary member working for my country.

I liked to make things with my hands. I could craft things easily, for this my neighbors praised and sometimes envied me.

One day I was sitting next to my father, trimming a branch from a trifoliate orange tree. At that time a visitor walked up to us. He looked at me working and said, "Oh, you cute boy! You have very skillful hands!" He picked up the slingshot I made and examined it in detail. And he said, "Let me buy this. Here is the money for you." I was embarrassed, but my father smiled and nodded at me to accept it. Since then my hand-made toys were sold occasionally.

Schoolwork was not interesting to me, because I had already learned Hangul (the Korean alphabets) and the multiplication table from my older brothers and sisters before I entered elementary school. I preferred playing outside to studying at home. I enjoyed playing physical games such as combat games, wrestling and kicking, and in those games I led my team. I was comparatively strong and competitive, so I could not endure losing. When I lost, my self-esteem was hurt and my pride made me play until I could win. Losing was not my way.

I was born very strong and my parents fed me some tonic medicines. Therefore I was called 'Mr. Strong' or 'Gorilla.' Although my parents were not rich and had many kids, they bought those medicines for me, their youngest son, because I was their favorite.

My Mother

I cannot forget this. After this, my mother seemed to love me much more.

I was five years old. It was a very busy time with everyone helping with the harvest in the fields. I was watching my house alone. Suddenly the sky became dark and it began to rain. There were peppers laid out in the front yard to dry. Although I was quite young, I thought I must do something to keep them from getting wet. So I hurried to pick them up with my tiny fingers. At that time my mother, worrying over the peppers even when it dripped, was running into the house. She was very happy to see me doing that.

"Oh, my baby, Jaerock! You're grown up! How smart you are to pick these up! I love you so much, baby!"

I still remember vividly my mother's eyes containing a deep love for me, as she patted my butt with her hand. She would say about me, her youngest son trying to help her, (as Korean mothers do) 'I wouldn't feel any pain, although I physically put my baby into my eye.'

She always saved a portion for me if there was any good food.

When I went out with my mother, holding her hand, my elderly neighbors who were recreating themselves with games and chatting in the resting-place next to a big tree, used to say, "Oh, sweetie! You look very bright. You will be something in the future." "His face says he'll be a big person. Please take good care of him, ma'am."

Their greetings and comments made my mother happy and proud of me. She often rubbed my head with her hand.

One night I saw my mother dress up in white clothes after a bath. I thought she was getting ready to go out, so I asked her to take me. To go out with her was my pleasure all the time. I enjoyed looking around the open market area, riding on the bus, and eating delicious foods with my mother.

"I want to come with you, Mom."

"Jaerock, I'm not going out. I'm going to pray to the Big Dipper for you (my youngest son), your brothers and sisters to grow up healthy and to be great. You go ahead to bed, baby."

I watched her praying to her god, putting a bowl of water on a small table pot in the backyard, and rubbing her palms together for a long time. I was a little child, but I could feel a deep gratitude for her praying for me.

Praying to the Big Dipper

How great was her parental love? But now, she says to me, 'You'd better die.' because I am sick too much (as an adult), not as her baby son. My sorriness about my life became greater as time went on.

Can I no longer play on the hillside where I used to play when I was a child? Despite my mother's prayers to her Big Dipper every night, all I have now is poverty and a sick body. I hate my sick body. How come I cannot be healthy like others, and how come I cannot get out of this tunnel of pain?

I was proud of my health, but now I'm suffering from diseases. I memorized everything that I learned, and I was told I was smart. But now, I can do nothing. No one is able to predict even one minute of the future! Even my own parents are abandoning me. Who will, then, take care of me from now on?

I was unaware that hot tears were streaming down my face. I did not try to wipe them off but kept weeping. How long had I been crying? I saw my mom walk into the room with a bowl of boiled medicine that smelled terrible to me. Then my sorriness for her disappeared, and my heart was filled with pity.

It was a long hard time of suffering, but she devoted herself to curing me. But my illness got worse, and I showed no hope of recovery. I could understand why she said to me, 'You'd better die.'

I received the bowl of medicine silently from my mother. 'I must stay alive. To stay alive I must take this medicine. I will revive.' Deciding to survive, I lifted up the bowl and drank it to the bottom slowly.

'Oh, wonderful days, come back to me! Come back to me!'

The struggle

Shadow of misfortune

My schooldays at elementary, middle and high school went easily. Comparatively, my life, after I entered college and when I completed my military duty, began to be mixed with a bitter taste.

After I finished military service, I was supposed to get back to my college, but I could not afford it. I had lost all my inherited property. A swindler deceived me and ate up all my money. It was my fault to trust her in this deceitful world. She took advantage of my deep trust in her. Her betrayal axed my feet so that I could not take any steps forward. It ruined my future.

I spent several months in disappointment and frustration until my pen pal aggressively proposed to me. After my niece introduced her to me, we corresponded and dated for three years. Neither my parents nor hers agreed to our marriage. So our wedding was not a normal one that is traditionally blessed by both families.

In spite of all this, we set up our love nest and planned to live our new life together. We thought of people who had succeeded by overcoming hardships and failures. We set up plans for our promising future - I would go to work at a newspaper during the daytime and study at night. My wife would open a small beauty parlor.

Drank too much

It was one day in spring. I was semi-forced by my friends to hold a party for celebrating a job and marriage.

In the morning I enjoyed a party with my co-workers, then luncheon with college friends, and in the evening dinner and drinks with my hometown friends. We enjoyed ourselves for the first time in a long while, drinking several rounds of alcohol. I was very pleased with my friends who gave us congratulatory comments on our wedding. Their encouragement seemed to bring me new hope for a new life.

In the meantime the shadow of misfortune was approaching nearer and nearer, unknown to me.

The party was over right before (There was a nationwide curfew at that time from midnight to four a.m.) on that night. I felt a little relief for the day, thinking that the party went well to the end. Suddenly I felt dizzy. Every object in the room began to spin around me. I could not keep my body balanced. I fell in and out of consciousness, and kept vomiting until my body twisted because of the severe pain. It made my wife so scared that she rushed out to a drug store. She got some medicine for me, but I could not swallow anything, even water. I threw up everything I had. My vomiting continued overnight until only yellowish water came up. My pain was extremely severe, as if my intestines were forcefully drawn up to my throat.

I was used to drinking alcohol since I was a child. When I accidentally had my ribs hurt, my parents fed me special liquor made with a snake. This snake-liquor medicated my wounds better and better, and it trained my body to be strong against alcohol. Since then, I became proud of my strength against alcohol, and it caused my friends to nickname me 'Mr. Alcohol.'

When I drank with my friends at the party, the alcohol was a very strong kind of liquor, whiskey. On the previous night I had bought forty 720-ml bottles, and my friends brought even more liquor.

(I later figured out how much I drank that day. It would be about five bottles.)

As the host of the party, I was not supposed to reject any toast. So, not to get drunk early I put some sugar in my glass before I drank. I liked sweet things very much, and I was strong enough to beat everybody in drinking. Therefore, I had no problem at all that day, and kept drinking without any caution. It was too much, though. It was foolish of me not to notice myself getting hurt. I could have died. My stomach stopped functioning due to the alcohol that was too much and too strong. I was not made of iron.

That happened on a Sunday in March 1968.

My body was a storehouse of disease.

At first my wife and I did not worry about me too much. We thought I got sick because I drank so much. But the pharmacists' prescriptions did not make me get well. So, as a reporter, I chased down information all over seeking the best remedy. I tried several kinds of western and oriental medications. None of them worked. I had more serious problems. Day by day my digestion became poorer, and my body was getting skinnier.

I finally went to see a doctor at a big modern hospital, who said that I had nothing more serious than a little ulcer in my stomach. I received his treatments for a long time, but gained no recovery. During that time my body became weaker and weaker so that a lot of complications arose all over my body, such as stomach ulcer, poor appetite, weight loss, nervous breakdown, severe headache, pernicious anemia, sinusitis, ear infection, frostbite, athlete's foot, lymph inflammation, dermatitis and eczema. I had more diseases that I had never heard the names of before. I was like a storehouse of diseases.

One day my father took me to a famous herb doctor. He examined me completely and said, "This is a miracle. How could you still be alive?" He found that my sudden excessive drinking of liquor almost burnt my stomach and stopped its functioning. That is why I could not digest any food to nourish my body. My stomach and intestines could not absorb any nourishment for the organs to work. And thus my body lost the ability to fight against diseases. The malfunction of my stomach caused many complications to arise. No part of my body was left unaffected. My body looked like a war zone.

Fighting the diseases, I started my struggle to recover my health. It was a wretched and lonely fight.

Only if I can be healed

At first I earnestly followed the prescriptions that the pharmacists, herb doctors and modern medical doctors gave me. I would seem to recover from one disease, but another one took its place. For over one year I relied upon modern medical treatments. Unfortunately my condition continued to worsen.

I had to quit my job. I had no income, but my medical bills kept mounting. Consequently our living condition became miserable. However, I could not lose the fight against my diseases. I was unable to pay the hospital bills, and no doctor could cure me. So I had to find other ways to fight. If someone furnished me with an idea for a cure, I would borrow money to apply it.

"Go to a Buddhist temple, and worship Buddha for 100 days."

"Invite an exorcist to practice a shaman ritual."

"You'd better set an idol in your room."

"You must change your name."

I had identified myself as an atheist, but I tried to worship any godly being, hoping for a cure. One day I was told to take a bath, wear new clothes, and lie on the blanket. Then a chicken was placed next to my pillow as a ritual to cast away the bad ghost that had given me the diseases. My wife grabbed a knife, recited an incantation, and with full concentration she rushed forward to stab the chicken with a knife.

Now I think it was ridiculous. Unless you have suffered, you would not understand we had no choice but to try everything possible.

I ground my teeth in my efforts to stay alive. My wife and my mother brought whatever was suggested to be helpful and gave it to me. I ate simmered centipedes, motherwort, the skin of a lacquer tree, cat meat, even the gall bladders of a dog and a bear, and drank liquor in which a snake was steeped.

Three years later I had a problem in my legs. When I walked, I felt extreme pain in my knees, so I could not stand for any length of time. The doctor said it was rheumatoid arthritis. After I tried several medications with no results, I heard that cat meat was good for rheumatoid arthritis. At that time my wife was working in a market in Gumho-dong. Whenever she saw a cat, she bought and boiled it for me. If the cat meat was boiled improperly, the smell would almost make me vomit when I tried to eat it.

I cannot imagine how many cats I ate. No more did cats exist in Sungdong-gu area, so we had to go to Namdaemun Market and Joongboo Market to get cats. My only wish was to walk.

I even drank human excremental water

With the passing of time my condition became worse so that I could no longer get to the bathroom by myself. I needed someone to empty my waste for me. It was then that a man showed up. He was like a savior to me.

"Do you want to stay alive? I know one way for you."

"What is it? Please tell me!"

"You were beaten a lot when you were young, weren't you? The dead blood accumulated in your body, and it caused you to get sick. Only the excremental water, filtered through pine needles in the septic tank, will cure you."

My mother and my wife were almost dancing with joy, and my chest swelled with hope. We hurried ourselves down to my hometown. My mother set the pine needles in the mouth of a pot and put the pot into the septic tank. The next day she pulled the string to remove the pot. Some water had accumulated in the pot overnight. Mom poured out that water into a bowl and cautiously brought the bowl to me with two hands.

I drank the water three times a day for fifteen days without missing any doses. In spite of the horrible smell I managed to drink each dose. If I tried to drink the water directly from the bowl, it made me throw up. So I drank it with a straw to avoid tasting it on my tongue. It went directly down my throat but still smelled terrible. I had to brush my teeth for about ten minutes and suck on candies, but my mouth still did not feel clean.

My struggle with the diseases was not over yet. I finally got very potent German-made pills that were used for leprosy patients. They said the pills were the only medicine able to cure the skin diseases, which were spread all over my body. I thought only if I can be cured, why not? Excremental water or leprosy medication, I'll try it.

My struggle in vain

My struggles resulted in misery. I learned two important facts: one was that in this world there are diseases impossible to cure with any medical science, any god or any ancient remedy. The other was that my body was totally wretched and destroyed beyond repair.

I missed my strong legs and healthy ears. I really desired to get my clean body and clear mind back. Regardless of my desire for health, the goddess of death beckoned to me, pulling me to the threshold of death.

My struggle began to lose its strength like a butterfly whose wings are cut off. Only my pride, which never allowed anyone to beat me, kept me alive, fighting with death. Although this terrible long fight had completely exhausted me, I knew my struggle was not yet over.

As time passes by

My wife, head of our family

Like someone trying to escape a swamp, the more I struggled, the deeper I sank. My struggle brought more diseases and drove my home to starvation.

My wife devotedly took care of me, her sick husband, in spite of having a very short honeymoon. She was more than wise and very capable. If she heard of something helpful to me, she got it to feed me. No matter how hard it was to obtain it, or how far she had to go to get it, she was willing to do this for me. Nothing was impossible or too shameful for her to do for my recovery.

Occasionally when something hurt her feelings, she got mad and packed her belongings to go to her parents. She was sometimes a hot-tempered woman. For several years I had not shown any improvement in my health, and so my wife often left home. These circumstances led to a terrible phase in my home's economy. My wife had to borrow more money to pay back the previous debts. When my wife was too much pressed by the creditors, she ran from our home, asking for a divorce. To look at my wife leaving me was enough to tear out my heart. Thankfully, in most cases my wife came back within a few days.

One day she returned home with a bright face.

"Honey, my older sister gave me 100,000 Won (US $ 83). With this money I'm going to open a shop in the market."

Some days later she opened a store in Gumho Market. She started her life as the head of our family. In her store she sold Kimbap (the cooked rice wrapped with dry seaweed), donuts, bread, fried foods, noodles and even alcoholic drinks. She left home early in the morning to buy ingredients for the snack foods and returned home right before midnight. She worked long hours to make as much money as possible.

I usually stayed home alone, reading books and enjoying my dreams. When I felt too bored, I stepped out to the three-way intersection where I sat on the wooden seat-table, watching the people play Badook (the territory game playing with black and white rocks) or Hwatoo (a Korean card game).

Who would understand me, who had no choice but to spend time worthlessly like that, when I should be the head of my house?

My poor daughters

I had two daughters, adding to my heartache. My first daughter, Miyoung grew, always seeing me sick. She was born good-hearted. She always helped me, sometimes as my hands and feet, and sometimes as a friend. If she went out, she did not stay out for a long time so that I would not worry about her. I was sorry that many diseases infected her skin as well, and she often got sick because we were unable to care for her properly.

My second daughter, Mikyoung, whom I rarely saw, was sent to my mother. Mikyung was weaned when her mother opened a store. She grew up under her grandmother's care in the countryside. Her face was mine. My other family members did not like her because she reminded them of me, their mutual headache (a long sick family member). She was almost abandoned, and she had to play alone. When I saw her biting a dirty rug in her mouth, my heart hurt desperately.

Even though Mikyung was too young to leave us, my wife sent her to the countryside, and worked even harder to earn more money. She knew that I would die before I asked my parents for help. She had to manage our living and pay for my medicines and the daily-increasing debts. She was asked to pay back the creditors, and at the same time she had to seek new sources she could borrow money from to pay the interest. She earned some money, but it was too little to cover the daily interest on the money we borrowed. Our home economy was undoubtedly getting worse and worse. I hated myself, because I couldn't do anything for my wife who overworked everyday.

One day, being extremely harassed by the creditors, my wife complained to me. "What are you, huh? I don't believe this. Are you a man? I married you. How can you have me go out to earn money? I don't need your love. I need money! Give me money!"

She looked insane. She cried. She ripped away my pride and left home. She did not come back home for a while. Miyoung eagerly looked for her mom. "Daddy, why doesn't Mom come home? Is she at the store working? Let's go see her, Daddy."

When she handed me the stick standing in the corner of my room, she was crying. I couldn't take it any more. I told her to go get a bottle of liquor and a pack of cigarettes. I drank. I drank to forget my guilt for burdening my wife too much, to get rid of the hatred for my wife, and not to feel the pain of my own. I drank and drank, ignoring my sick body.

'When my mother said to me, "You'd better die," I said to myself, "Stay alive!" I did try everything to revive. But now, even my wife abandoned me. My wife left me!'

As time passes by

My cigarette smoke drifted up in the air, faded away and disappeared for good. Consequently my heart also left my wife. And my aspiration for life was disappearing. 'Okay, now, everybody has left me! I have liquor, though. It will help me forget the pain. And my cigarette will comfort my sadness. No problem!'

My wife came back and coldly stated, "I came back not to see you but Miyoung. Don't misunderstand." I felt miserable for myself listening to this kind of cold statement and not responding, as her husband should. I was sorry for her vicious attitude toward me.

From that moment, my health rapidly got worse. I did not feel like striving for life, because no one liked me. So I decided to live for my own convenience. I had no will to live a normal life. I just let life pass me by.

I kept drinking and smoking to ease my anger against those who abandoned me. I could not choose to die.

'How foolish was I? I seemed to have no backbone. I got sick because of drinking. My illness drove my parents, brothers, sisters and friends to abandon me. So I considered alcohol as my enemy. For now, however, I'm trying to find comfort with alcohol as my friend. How ironic is this?'

At my dining table some kind of alcohol was always present. If I did not drink, I could not do anything because my hands trembled and I felt unstable. I could not eat any food without alcohol. I was becoming an alcoholic.

My life was lived one day at a time. I had no concept of tomorrow in my consciousness. I was a dayfly. One day was painful enough. How could I look forward to tomorrow, which would be just as painful as today? I drank more and more to forget the pain of each day. My health was being destroyed. And my living was out of control like a leaf afloat on the water in a flowing stream.

I was too foolish

I was more than foolish. I regret that I unthinkingly wasted those days. I should have paid attention to my life. 'Once time has gone, it never comes back. Why have I managed my precious time and life this wretchedly? I should've tried to endure the pain of my life wisely. I shouldn't look at the present pain but look to the hope of the future. God helps those who help themselves. Every cloud has a silver lining.'

As I gave up the will to survive, my life became an endless stream of meaningless days. With no conscious thought I ate, drank and slept like a wild animal. I had no complaints and no hope. To be alive each day was good enough to me, and I became accustomed to living this way. How foolish was I?

Everybody faces death sooner or later, eventually going over the threshold of death. They say that the happiest death is dying quickly before feeling any pain. Unfortunately I spent seven long years at the doorstep of death, neither alive nor dead. Time flowed like a stream, but my life was moving backward with my heart frozen. I was like Jonah who was imprisoned inside a fish in the deep sea.

2
THE MIRACLE

Affection

Affection is a word that means giving kindness and warmth. Affection is shown between neighbors who interact with each other. Parents have affection toward the children they have borne and raised. Another affection is between mother-in-law and daughter-in-law, being mixed with hatred and obligation to some degree. So you can tell people live by affection.

What is affection then? The dictionary says, 'Affection is the kind and loving expression of the heart between people.' To say briefly, affection is a kind of love mankind gives. Man is a social animal. From your birth you must live with others. You can grow by the milk and love supplied by your mother. If you get milk supplied but love is withheld, you are apt to grow up to be a problem to society due to lack of love.

Affection is given and received from many sources. At home when you are a child, at school as a student, and in the workplace as a community member. Another type of affection is given and received between loved ones, spouses, and between parents and children. Likewise, people as social animals live their lives, giving and receiving affection until death. Everybody needs affection to live a worthy life.

During my seven miserable years of life standing at the doorstep of death, I learned how to analyze whether the affection shown within different relationships was true or false. I came to know that affection is not true love.

Affection between acquaintances

Through exchanging pen pal letters I came to know my present wife. When I was young, I was outgoing. As I grew older, my bad-looking teeth made me become shy and quiet with an introspective nature. I did not show interest in any girl. So when I met my wife for the first time, I could not talk well, although we talked a lot through our letters.

"I, I... My name is Jaerock Lee."

"My name is Boknim Lee."

Although it was the first meeting between us, we could feel something like affection arising in ourselves. Since then we called each other 'Brother' or 'Sister', thus cultivating our love. If we had not said greetings when we first met, and just kept quiet with no conversation or talked without opening our hearts, we would not have felt affection.

My niece, who introduced my wife to me as a pen pal, was surprised to hear of us. She had wanted to help me make a pen pal for fun, not for love. She discouraged us from getting married.

Affection between husband and wife

We made a promise to get married. I liked her active, good and compassionate personality, and she liked my straight, warm-hearted and sensitive personality. We needed each other, and we were beneficial to each other. We decided to be united as one flesh, so we got married.

A short time after we had been married, I suddenly got sick. I had to quit my job due to my illness, so I was not able to manage our living. My wife had affection for me as her spouse. She did everything possible to find a remedy for me and worked hard to manage our living. If she did not have affection for me, she would have run away or would not have devoted herself to me at all.

However, if she had truly loved me as her husband, she would not have done anything to make my heart ache.

"I'm going to get divorced from you. Not now, though. If I do now, everybody will talk badly about me, saying, 'She kicked her husband when he was sick.' When you get cured, I'll get a divorce."

I could feel that she did not love me in her heart any longer. She just tried to maintain our marital status because the others might speak badly of her. Her love became cold, as I could not give her any benefit but could only be a burden to her. If she had had true spousal love, she would have endured any pain and made any sacrifice. She would not have behaved rudely and she would not have hurt my heart.

Affection between parents and children

A man and a woman united in flesh beget a child as the fruit of their love. That is why they say the affection between parents and children cannot be cut off. When my mother, who had loved me so much when I was a child, told me to die, I came to realize that there is no true love between parents and children.

There is an old saying, "Long sickness can't make a good son." My long sickness could not make my parents nice to me, either. Far from being a good son, I was dying of diseases. My father kept away from me because he worried his social status would be hurt by me. And my mother told me to die because she could not endure the pain in her heart any longer. I do not think my parents had true love for me. If so, they would not have wanted me to die, even if I had been heavily handicapped or I had committed a grave crime.

Coming to a dead-end

I could not find a true friend among my friends. A friend in need is a friend indeed. When I was suffering from illness, I realized that it is hard to find a true friendship. Some of my friends helped me a lot, seeking remedies here and there. However, when they thought I had no hope of recovery, all of them left me. Friendship is good but not always permanent.

What about my brothers? Could they give me true love after our parents gave up on me? In my home village we were said to have a wonderful brotherhood. My brothers said to me,

"Jaerock, don't worry. We'll back you up, brother. No worry, OK?" Then they did not keep their word. They stopped helping me financially, when they realized that to aid me would be like trying to fill a bottomless pot with water.

People live their lives loving each other. I see a lot of people stop loving someone when they cannot receive love from that person. Can this be a true love? Through my seven years of suffering I came to know that affection between people in this world was not a true love. I was sad to know this:

Affection is a love of mankind.
Affection is not a true love.
Affection is a love that changes.
Affection is not a sincere love.
True love is the love that you would die for.
True love never changes.
True love did not exist in this world.
It was not in parents.
It was not between husband and wife.
It was not among brothers.
It was not between parents and children.
It was not in friendship, either.

Sick body and broken heart

In March 1968, a nightmarish incident happened to me. A few hours of enjoyment snatched my health, and it never returned to me. I started out celebrating a job and marriage, and then the pain of disease was all that remained. I drank strong liquor too much, and it killed my stomach so that it stopped functioning.

My body getting sick

My stomach stopped functioning, causing all my organs to become weaker and weaker. Vomiting, dizziness, indigestion and headache attacked me frequently. New symptoms arose causing me to also suffer from loss of appetite, fatigue, rashes, itching and no motivation or energy. But that was not all. My mouth was full of ulcers, and colds and coughs did not leave me because my resistance was weakened. I had an infection in one ear that continuously drained.

When I was in fourth grade, there was a teacher nicknamed 'Mr. Crazy.' One day he saw me play the game 'Sabee' with my friend. He thought we were fighting. He called us over and charged us to hit each other on the cheek without asking any question. There was no reason for me to hit my friend, so I just kept standing. Then Mr. Crazy crazily slapped me on the face. I was shocked to be treated like that by a teacher. And I had my eardrum ruptured. Afterwards Mr. Crazy was kicked out of the school.

Since that time I had had a hearing problem, so I had to watch the speaker's lips very carefully. Unless I was sure what the speaker said, I did not respond. It became my new habit. Sometime later, a problem developed in the other ear. The infection worsened, drained more, and smelled bad. Eventually I could not hear gentle sounds. When someone called me from behind or when I talked on the phone, I was embarrassed because I could not hear well. When I talked to someone face to face, I broke into a cold sweat. When my phone rang, I left the room because my heart started pounding. Then people began to give me strange looks, so that I felt I was being treated like a fool, and a feeling of inferiority captured me.

A kind of nervous breakdown was settling on me. I had to quit my job as a newspaper man and could not get a new job. I was almost deaf, so I could not play normal roles in my community.

In summer, athlete's foot and in winter, frostbites on the ears and feet, developed, bothering me terribly. The itchiness was too irritating for me to endure. To make matters worse, my entire body itched and rashes appeared all over. When I got up in the morning, I found that pus had oozed from my boils. My wife had verbally abused me so many times that I did not dare tell her about the boils. These boils spread all over my body, and the inflammation became worse and worse, so that I could no longer hide them from my wife. "You have only one healthy part, your eyes. How nice that is! What kind of person are you to have all kinds of dirty diseases?"

Even in my nose I had a problem. I had not noticed that I had a sinus infection. Always my head felt heavy, my nose was stuffy, and I was losing my ability to remember.

Of course my neck could not be normal. In the beginning my lymph node was swollen, and later I felt something solid in it. The solid mass grew to the size of a bean and then increased to the size of a grape. The mass pressed on my neck, so whenever I turned my head, I felt pain.

Although I had a lot of diseases, my clothes could hide my skin diseases. I might have looked weak to other people, but they would have treated me as a healthy man unless the rheumatoid arthritis affected my knees. In 1972, I began to feel pain in my knees when I walked. Soon I was unable to walk. I had to rely on a stick to help me get to the bathroom. Eventually I needed someone to empty my waste for me.

It was hard for me to bear my physical pain because I used to have a very healthy body. But a worse pain was to follow, which was a mental one that nobody could understand.

I could not hear

As a sick man I had a lot of sorrow. My sorrow was derived from my inability to hear. Although I carefully watched the lips of the speaker, if I was in a noisy coffee shop or crowded places, I could not catch what they said. So I sometimes responded with wrong answers or could not answer. Then I felt shame accompanied with the feeling of inferiority.

I had a fierce pride, so I tried to hide my inability to hear. That made me feel pain. Even my eldest brother, living in the same house for some months, did not know I could not hear well. He was a kind of hot-tempered man, so he could not understand why I, his younger brother, watched his lips and talked very slowly. He often slapped me because I could not hear him well.

I could not eat

Some people say, 'Business after pleasure.' Eating is very essential to human beings. What will happen if one does not eat? Everyone has the instinctive desire to eat. If you lose the pleasure of eating, you will not feel any joy in your life.

Sometimes I felt a strong desire to eat meat. Then my wife cooked some specially prepared tender meat for me. Although she pounded and partially cut the meat, it often remained in my stomach to cause intense pain. However, after a short while, that desire to have meat came to me again. I could not force myself to eat the meat though, remembering that severe pain.

"Honey, when can I eat the meat with rice as much as I want?"

My wife knew that day would never come. But she said confidently, "Don't worry. Someday you can eat as much as you want. Then I'll show you my best recipe. But don't eat too much."

I could not eat well, so my weight dropped lower and lower and my face became skinnier and skinnier. When I looked in the mirror, "Oh, no, who is this?" I asked aloud. Big eyes, prominent cheekbones, sunken cheeks, filthy ears and rough skin... It was impossible to see my original features among those.

I could not walk

To breathe fresh air, I could step outside for a while, relying on a stick to walk. When I became unable to walk at all, my life was like a prison with no windows. To stay only in the room was too stuffy for me at such a young age. I felt deeply miserable because I had no place to work, although I desired a job. I could not do anything as the head of the family or as a husband. This gave me a feeling of guilt pressing down on my heart.

However, my wife did not understand what I was feeling. She often tore my heart to pieces.

I could not make any money

Our creditors had hounded my wife. Her love for me gradually cooled. She was becoming a slave to money. She believed that money is the answer to all misfortune. But she used to say that she was happy only for my love.

"Money makes me happy. I need money, not you! Unless you make money, don't boss me around, OK? You brought all these hardships with you, all these!"

Every time she ran out, she never came back by herself unless I went to pick her up. She lived with me not because she loved me as her husband, but because she was obligated as my wife. When I realized the fact that she stayed with me just because of the affection for our children, my heart was deeply cut and it was impossible to cure. Thus my love for her cooled, and deep sorrow took its place instead.

My heart was torn to pieces

The pain my wife gave me was bearable, because it was all

based on the money. The unbearable pain, however, came from the wrath of my wife's family toward me. She must have listed all of her complaints about me in front of her family while she was staying with them after she ran out.

"See, we told you, 'Don't get married to him.' Why did he want to marry you that eagerly? He must have been sick before he married you. If not, how come he can't work and make money now?"

"He cheated you!"

"He's a liar! A bold-faced liar!"

Finally my wife's family showed up all together and complained to me.

"Hey, you cripple, son-in-law! Talk to me, what's wrong with my daughter? Why did you hit my daughter?" They exaggerated our altercation and said I hit her.

"Hey, brother-in-law, why don't you just get a divorce? I think you both will be better off."

"Are you a man? How could you let your wife work that hard? Hasn't she done enough?"

"You, stupid cripple! Don't say anything! We demand you to get a divorce, right now!"

They yelled at me loud enough for my neighbors to hear, then left me, as if they had done nothing wrong. How contemptuous and how hurtful! It is beyond what words can describe. They knew nothing about my heart. They just looked at my sick body and treated me as a cripple. They never tried to understand how I felt in sickness. They just hurt me, complaining that I was of no help to them. What they did to me was inhuman. It was not affection. It was not love.

When I got ill, people left me one by one. At first they kicked me out of their hearts and then abandoned me. I was so hurt to see I was being forgotten and abandoned. No one came to comfort me. When they heard I was sick, they came to give me pity and some help. But when they knew that I had no hope of recovery, everybody left me alone. No one truly loved me. If they left me something, it was my incurably hurt and torn heart.

What would you do, if one of your parents or spouse has been ill for years? How would you treat your parent or spouse, if he (she) was a leper or an AIDS patient? Would you turn your face away, because you get only a headache from the person? Would you harass the person verbally and spiritually and tear at his (her) heart, because he (she) gives you only pain? Or would you take care of the person out of obligation, because he (she) is one of your family members? Or will you take care of him (her) with human warmth and love, willingly sacrificing yourself?

It would not be easy to do with human love, but with the love of God you would be able to overcome any hardship.

Love is patient, love is kind and is not jealous; love does not brag and is not arrogant, does not act unbecomingly; it does not seek its own, is not provoked, does not take into account a wrong suffered, does not rejoice in unrighteousness, but rejoices with the truth;

bears all things, believes all things, hopes all things, endures all things (1 Corinthians 13:4-7).

Immortal wretched life

I had attempted to commit suicide two times. I failed in both attempts. I was on the brink of death because I could not eat. My life seemed as if it never ends.

First attempt to commit suicide

Up to twelfth grade I was often absent from school because I accidentally hurt my ribs while playing the kicking game with a middle school student when I was in fourth grade. My pride did not allow me to rely on any other person for any reason. I was too shy to reveal that I was hurt. The pain in my body became more intense, and it forced me to be absent many times from my high school. My grades fell so much that I gave up trying to enter college that year, so I decided to apply for Seoul National University next year.

My second year to prepare for college admission gave me a worthy opportunity to test my abilities. I slept no longer than four hours a day. To stay awake I took some pills. And I even set up my own rules to punish myself for getting up late in the morning.

If I did not get up at the sound of the alarm, I started to count 1... 2... 3... If I passed 3, I did not eat breakfast. So, not to be starved, I got up on time. Every morning I went to the public library to study for the college entrance exam. Because I studied so hard, I improved day by day. I enjoyed studying, and I was happy because I was sure that I would be entering the College of Engineering, Seoul National University.

One day something strange happened to me. Of course I did not know this proverb: *"The mind of man plans his way, But the LORD directs his steps"* (Proverbs 16:9).

During a break I was reading a newspaper, but I could not remember the president's name, whose photo I was looking at. 'What was his name?' I just could not remember. 'What's wrong with me? Why can't I remember?' I strained to remember his name, but I could not get it.

'Oh, Yeah... Yi... His last name is Yi. Why isn't his first name coming to me? Perhaps I've studied too hard. How could I forget such a common thing?'

Feeling a little strange, I was getting lost. So, I tried to memorize what I studied. 'A mathematical formula... what about factorization?' Nothing. 'Uh, what's happening to me? I can't remember even the simple things!' An ominous presence hit me.

'What about the National Language?' I tried to memorize an ancient poem. But I could not remember the name of the poet or the title of it. I was shocked and afraid. 'What's wrong with me? Have I lost all my memory? Or am I just being absent-minded? How can this possibly happen?' I could not go to sleep all night long.

The next day, I tested myself again, whether or not I would

be able to remember those things I had studied for months. I could remember nothing, no matter how hard I tried to. I felt like I was falling into a deep pit. I began to question the value of my life, and it shocked me. I realized that I had no reason to live in this world.

'It would be better if I were dead. Then I wouldn't disappoint my parents by not fulfilling their desires. How shameful if I fail to enter college after trying twice?'

I thought my death would solve everything. I stopped in all the drug stores in Uljiro Street to buy sleeping pills. I bought twenty pills. I took out my diary. Burning my diary page by page, I looked back on the whole twenty years of my life. I arranged my personal belongings, and I said good-bye to my life. I set up the D-day and a detailed plan for killing myself.

During the time I was studying, I lived in a rented room located near my eldest sister's house where I ate every meal. I shared the room with my elder brother, who usually came back from work at around 11 o'clock. Until he got back home, I stayed there alone. So, it was a good place for me to commit suicide.

I cleaned up my room, and I left my suicide notes to my parents, brothers and sisters. My plan was perfectly plotted, just waiting for the signal.

According to my plan, I first went to my elder sister's house.

"Sister, I'm going to study at my friend's tonight. You don't have to wait for me for dinner, OK?"

My generous sister believed me and kept on doing her

chores.

I returned to my room, put my shoes inside the room, and locked up the door. I spread a blanket, and I swallowed the twenty sleeping pills that I had prepared. It did not make me fall asleep for a little while. After I lay on the blanket, I lost consciousness.

That night my brother-in-law and elder brother felt a strange pull to return home earlier than their usual closing time of 11 o'clock. They closed their shop and came straight home, skipping their routine stop for a drink. They came to my room looking for me although they were told that I was at my friend's. They usually left me alone so as not to interrupt my studying. But that night they came to my room, and found it locked. Feeling uneasy, they broke in and found me lying like a corpse. They rushed me to the hospital right away. I had taken too many pills and too much time had passed so that, according to the doctor, it was impossible for me to revive. However, in a few days I regained consciousness. And soon I could go back to my normal life. Everyone said my revival was a miracle.

I realized that the old saying was true, 'Life and death are providential.' Because of this experience, I decided to take the college entrance exam. Anyhow I had to do my best. Persistently I applied for my long time goal, the College of Engineering at Seoul National University. I failed, so applied for the College of Engineering at Hanyang University and passed.

This is the story of my first attempt to commit suicide.

My second attempt to commit suicide

I tried to kill myself one more time.

When I was ill, no one took care of me. Even my wife ran out. So I wished for death at any time. I bought and collected sleeping pills for that purpose. When my wife abandoned me, my last hope was crushed. I took sleeping pills and waited for death.

I was a diehard. My wife, who was staying at her parents', could not go asleep that night. She felt uncomfortable about something at our house. Her uneasy feeling drove her to catch a taxi to go check on me, while I was dying. Thus, my second attempt failed.

'No matter how hard I try, I can't die. Then I won't foolishly try to kill myself any more. My life is not of my own but providential. I am like the bird that never dies.'

Since then I got a strong aspiration to live. In my deepest place the kindling of life started a fire. My attempts to die unexpectedly brought me a strong desire to stay alive. I did not think of committing suicide anymore.

I lived to avenge

When I was ill, many people harassed me. My own mother, my other half (my wife), my family members and relatives... the more they harassed me, the more tenaciously I wanted to survive.

Like the lava exploding out of the volcano, I had something hot in the bottom of my heart with which I would get revenge upon them.

"Mother, why should I die? I'll show you. You will see me healthy in the future!"

"Honey, I'll get you more money than you would ever want. You just wait until that time! You will be sorry!"

"Mother-in-law, don't treat me like that. You will regret it!"

What would happen to my daughters if I die?

I had another reason to survive.

My daughters... how miserably were they raised because I was sick? I had to live to compensate my daughters for their loss. I was a bad father to them. When I was sick and my heart hurt, I often got mad at them. I mistreated them in anger instead of showing love. Mostly I thought of them as irritating.

'They should grow by love. If I die, who would give them love? I must stay alive to fulfill my duty as a father. While I was still living, they mistreated and harassed my daughters. If I die, how much more contemptuous treatment would they get as single-parented children? Besides, my second daughter, who was weaned too early, was separated from her parents. My wife doesn't care for her. Who else will take care of her after I die?

I should stay alive for myself first. My life is my own. No one can live for me. Staying alive, I should do my job as a father and as a husband. I should live to pay back those to whom I was a burden.'

I firmly made up my mind to stay alive.

To make my home sweet and happy, I must stay alive to fulfill my duty. If I keep my consciousness, I can come back alive from the den of the tiger. I began to feel a strong aspiration to live, after being so close to death. I gained a hope to live a good worthy life.

The long seven years of my life in the valley of death consequently brought me hope for a better future.

My elder sister

When frogs were waking from their winter sleep and cold wind withdrew in the presence of golden bells blooming, spring came also to me.

1974 was my seventh year living a wretched life in the valley of death. I felt an urge from the deep place in my heart to go out somewhere to enjoy this spring.

No family members or any other visitors had come to see me.

One day my second eldest sister came to see me. I was so pleased to see her. It was like finding an oasis in the desert. I had really missed people and their love.

My elder sister came to see me

My second eldest sister was farming in our hometown. Sometimes she came up to see her children who were attending school in Seoul. It was a very busy time for farmers, so her visit surprised me.

"Oh, sister! What made you come up here?"

"I have something to do in Seoul, brother."

She looked so happy like a child. She talked to me about this and that which happened since we last met. We enjoyed talking for a long time. I was happy to see her excited. She stopped talking and cautiously asked me, "Brother, would you please do me a favor?"

I was curious because I would not be able to do anything for anybody.

"Didn't I tell you before? I really want to visit a place in Seoul. That is the Hyun Shinae Prayer House located in Sodaemoon. Your brother-in-law permitted me to go this time. Brother, would you please take me there?"

She sincerely asked a favor of me, expecting the pleasure to attend the meeting there. Her request was too earnest for me to say no. But I had to reject. "Sister, don't you know I can't? Why do you ask me that? You can get someone else to guide you. Why don't you go with Hyunkwon or Hyunsoo?"

She had two sons who could guide her. But she persistently asked me.

"Brother, I am a stranger to Seoul. And my kids have to go to school. I really want to go. That's why I'm asking you."

I could not say no to my elder sister. Besides, I also wanted to go out for a break. When I said, "Yes. I'll take you there," she was so pleased.

"How nice of you, brother! Thanks a lot. Get yourself ready tomorrow morning. I'll come here again, OK? I've got to go to cook dinner for my kids now."

As I watched her walk away, her steps looked like she was flying in joy. Her happy feature made me feel happy too, acknowledging myself, 'Oh, I can help others.'

My siblings were six in all. I was the youngest. I had two older brothers and three older sisters. Among them my second eldest sister was my favorite. Since birth, she was not only generous and warm-hearted, but also nice and diligent. So everybody liked her.

My second eldest sister, unfortunately, suffered from a fever when she was a baby. As a result she lost her sight in one eye. Her body was comparatively small. Her tiny features and a dead eye were made fun of by many people.

When she grew up to be a teenager, she was depressed by her appearance having a dead eye and small body. It drove her to make up her mind to stay single.

Some elderly neighbors with adult sons wanted her as their daughter-in-law. Thus she came to marry a man living in the neighboring village. After marriage she worked hard and managed the household well for her new family. She did her best for preparing their twelve memorial services a year. She gave birth to three sons and two daughters, and raised them with good care.

My elder sister accepted Jesus

One day a Christian elder living in the same village came to my elder sister and talked about the word of God. It gave her a genuine joy so that she really wanted to run to a church. At that time she was too busy to go to church due to her farming. Later on, a blind girl who was the daughter of a senior deaconess visited her to talk about Christianity. That blind girl came to see my sister everyday and talked about God. She was so earnest and her speaking was very interesting to my elder sister, who had a desire to keep listening to her story. Finally my elder sister went to her church. How happy and how joyful she felt! That day became unforgettable to my sister.

Since then, my elder sister has never missed going to church on Sundays. When she heard the sound of church bell, she hurried to finish her work to go to church. She always felt comfortable at church, and while she was working at home or in the field, she hummed hymns.

Although she was busy with farming, she spared as much time as she could to listen to the word of God. Whenever she went out to the field, she carried a radio in her basket. She tuned the radio to the Christian Broadcasting Station, and learned of hymnal songs and the word of God. Her life goals were to worship God, to evangelize to people, and to pray to God. Nothing else gave her any happiness.

In the farmers' busiest season, planting green rice, she kept every Sabbath Day. After she attended the late night prayer meetings, she never got up late the next morning. Getting up early and working hard, she always had a smile on her face. Her neighbors often said to her:

"I've never seen you get sick. If you believe in Jesus, can you live a healthy and happy life like that?"

Then she didn't miss the chance to spread the gospel to them.

She never left any work undone or put off before she went to church. Neither her husband's family nor any neighbor gave her a hard time relating to her Christian life. Only our mother and brothers gave her a hard time. Our mother and brothers didn't like her serving her church so earnestly and trying to evangelize to as many people as possible.

Every Sunday she got up early and finished all of the housing chores. Then she went to church and cleaned the altar before the service started. When she got the first harvest, she brought some and put it secretly into the pastor's house and ran away not to be seen. Our mother didn't like it and yelled at her for doing so.

"Do you have to give food to your church? They will rip you off. Stop going to church. Wake yourself up!"

Clicking her tongue, our mother scolded my sister. But it didn't make any difference. My sister responded, "Mom, please accept Jesus. Do you know how happy and joyful it is to believe in Jesus?"

My sister tried to spread the gospel whenever she had the chance. She believed that to have faith was more precious than richness or honor in this world. She earnestly prayed for her husband and children who did not go to church yet. She willingly endured all of the hardships and mistreatment given to her.

She offered a golden ring to God

When my sister heard of revivals, she always attended them. She loved God so much that she gave her most precious thing, a golden ring, to God. "Father, please give me the faith as precious as this golden ring. Please give me the faith like gold that never changes." She gave her golden wedding ring to God not for richness but for the golden faith.

My consent to guide gave her great joy. It vividly reminded me of her past days. She had often recommended going to church to me.

"Brother, you're living a new marriage life. Why don't you start your Christian life from now?"

It went in one ear and out the other. However, she tried to evangelize to me whenever we met. When I got sick, she came to see me.

"Sister, if I believe in Jesus, will I get healed? I don't think so. Who can heal my diseases that modern medical science couldn't cure? Where is God? Where is heaven? Did you ever see? I'm sorry to say this, sister. You have been deceived. It is easy to cheat you because you are naive. Never tell me again to go to church."

My cold response could not make my sister give me up. When she came up to Seoul, she insistently urged me to believe in Jesus. She was the only person who kept encouraging me during my wretched sick life, standing at the doorstep of death.

"Brother, it looks like you have nothing but death, right?

Listen, Brother. There is a way for you to survive. You can get your health back! Accept Jesus! That's the only way you should go!"

I did not try to go to church, but her earnest enthusiasm to evangelize to me made something grow in my mind: I might be healed, if I believe in Jesus. So I said 'yes' to guiding her, although I was exhausted mentally.

The wisdom God gave my elder sister

My sister's request for a guide was God's wonderful wisdom for leading me to a new life when I was standing at the doorstep of death. The living God, who chose the foolish to make them wise, and the poor to make them rich, gave my sister His wisdom. He opened the door to me, who was foolish and didn't know how to embrace life. God worked on me to answer my sister's earnest prayer:

"Father, please help my brother to meet you. Please heal him and let him glorify you. And let him evangelize to other family members to get salvation."

How could I, who was so foolish, realize God's wisdom, His wonderful wisdom to work on me? It came to me as a ray of light overcoming death. This ray of light protected and drove me to follow my sister's advice.

My second eldest sister is currently a senior deaconess at my church. She is serving the kingdom and righteousness of God as a devoted prayer warrior. Her daily life is for praying, evangelizing to people and thanking God. She is beloved and blessed by God so that she has strong faith and hope. She overcame hardship to live a victorious life. Her children grew up well and became servants of God, working for the world mission.

My reborn life

I went to the Hyun Shinae Prayer House

The next morning my elder sister came to my house to hurry me on. It took a long time for me to walk down the Gumho-dong hill, leaning on my stick.

Riding on a crowded bus, when we arrived at the Hyun Shinae Prayer House, their praises could be heard outside on the street.

"Come on, brother. We're late. Hurry, let's go in."

I was supposed to guide her in, but she guided me in.

Entering the building, I saw the second floor had no space for any people to sit. I tried to walk on the slope that was reserved for patients. Holding the railings, I took shuffling steps one by one to reach the third floor. I had pain in my knees and broke into a cold sweat.

Many people passed by me until I got myself into a position on the third floor. I was exhausted, so I took some time to catch my breath. Still lots of people came up and sat around me. I was wondering why so many people gathered here. When I looked around, I saw a woman wearing a white dress speaking at the microphone. She was preaching at the pulpit in an animated manner. A lot of people, raising their hands, were responding to her with 'Amen!' I felt heavy and fearful because I could not hear well and every feature was unfamiliar to me.

I could not see my elder sister who had been sitting next to me. I saw everybody around me start to pray in loud voices. Some of them, while praying, opened their mouths wide. They looked crazy to me. Some raised their hands, some shook their bodies, some cried and beat their chests, and some kept quiet with their mouths closed.

'What's wrong with these people? What kind of place is this? Why did I come here? I'd better get out of this place right away. Everybody looks crazy. If I stay longer, I'll get crazy too. I'll leave now.'

I had never been to a church. I thought believers would pray and behave quietly. But the people at the Hyun Shinae Prayer House were just the opposite of what I expected.

When I found my sister, I was disappointed with her behaviors. She was usually a shy person, but she was behaving like the other people, shaking her body, raising her hands, crying and praying. It was unbelievable.

'Is that my sister? I don't believe my eyes. Where is my quiet and shy sister?'

Thinking of her earnest request to come together, I could not ask her to go home. And I would not want to waste time looking around. When I looked at my sister acting so differently, I felt that a certain mysterious world might exist. So I knelt down like my sister. Closing my eyes, I put both hands together and began to pray.

At the time I prayed

Right then, my body became hot like fire, and I was soon soaked with hot sweat streaming down my back.

'Why am I suddenly sweating so much?' I was wondering; what's happening to me? At first I thought it's because of my shyness. (Later I knew that it was the fire of the Holy Spirit.)

I no longer felt fear or dislike. I became interested in what the praying lady in the white dress was uttering. Here, someone patted me on the shoulder. It was my sister.

"Hey, brother. It's time for us to receive her prayer. You are sick. Why don't you receive the prayer at the end? The final prayer is the most powerful."

She looked so happy, and her face was all smiles. While I was waiting for my turn to receive the prayer, I saw mysterious things. Some people were making their testimonies. They said that they almost died of illness but were healed after receiving the prayer there. They looked very sincere and full of rejoicing. They, giving all thanks and glory to God who forgave and healed them, even looked holy to me.

I'd like to receive the prayer

Everyone in the waiting line looked very sincere and faithful. It came to my turn. I bent my head for the prayer from Senior Deaconess Hyun. She laid her hand on my head, pressing down a little, patted me on the back, saying something, and pushed me away. I was pushed far from the place where I received her prayer. The floor was too slippery because so many people had been walking on it. I slipped and fell so that I felt ashamed when I got up.

'Is this prayer able to heal diseases?'

I looked doubtfully at the long waiting line of patients who were like POW's in custody. They reminded me of the Jungup Happenings, where a woman set up a fake healing assembly and deceived the patients. Her cohorts spread the rumor that she could heal any disease. That brought patients to Jungup City. Thousands of patients came there individually or in groups by chartered bus from all over the nation. She became very famous and was reported by newspapers as the healer of all kinds of diseases. However, it was found that she and her assistants cheated every patient with her false healing. She was arrested for fraud.

Thinking of the happening, I found myself standing on the ground floor. I did not know how I came down from the third floor without feeling any pain in my knees. My sister, who had fulfilled her long-awaited desire, was all smiles.

On the way back we took a bus, and I sat my exhausted body down on a seat. As I stared out the window unseeingly, something strange began to happen to me. Something like rolls of thunder sounded in my ears continuously. When I got off the bus at the Gumho-dong Market, I stopped hearing the thunderous sound.

'What sound did I hear on the bus? Why was the sound so

loud?' Looking up to the sky, I still wondered.

Getting into the market alley, we parted. My sister headed for her sons, and I headed for my wife's snack bar.

Honey, give me some rice

My wife managed a snack bar, taking responsibility for the family. She cooked and sold some noodles and fried foods. Her foods tasted good and brought many customers.

When I saw some food displayed, I felt a strong appetite. They looked so delicious that I asked for some, stepping into her snack bar.

"Honey, I'm very hungry. Give me some rice and meat. Please hurry."

"Did you say rice and meat? Are you crazy? The Hyun Shinae Prayer House made you like this? Don't you remember meat could kill you? Please wait. I'll cook something else for you instead."

She was busy working. I asked her again.

"Listen, honey. I feel like I can eat anything now. Don't worry about my digestion. Just give me a little meat, will you?"

She turned her face to me begging for meat like a baby. She looked at me for a while and reluctantly brought some meat and rice. My mouth watered so much at the sight of the food that my tongue enjoyed them like ice cream. I could not swallow any meat before, but that time I really enjoyed it and swallowed easily. I ate up a bowl of rice and a dish of meat very quickly. It made my wife's face worried.

"Are you okay, honey?"

It was 'business after pleasure' to me. I realized that eating is an essential pleasure for man to live. I leaned back against my chair to enjoy my feeling of fullness. Then I heard a very clear sound.

Honey, I hear now!

Without realizing it, I was talking to the customers sitting at the next table.

"Sir, what did you say just now? You ordered some food, right?"

"Yes, I did, Ttukbokki (spicy hot rice bar) for two people. Isn't it ready yet?" He responded to me, wondering why.

I was jumping for joy. I ran to my wife with a shout, "Honey, Ttukbokki for two!" I kept shouting. "Honey, I hear, I can hear now! I can hear what they say clearly! Very clearly!"

My rejoicing swelled my chest and made me cry. Hot tears were welling up in my eyes.

I could understand why I heard the thunder-like sound on the bus. I had heard the mixed sounds of the bus engine and passengers' talking. I had never anticipated that I would hear again with my fractured eardrums.

That night my wife and I were so happy that I could hear clearly. We could not figure out why I could hear. Feeling happy, I fell asleep sweetly. I thought I slept well because of being outside for the first time in years.

Every morning I started my day with a routine. Go to bathroom, wash my face, brush my teeth and then clean up my body here and there. I did these jobs alone so as not to show my dirty sores to my wife.

In the morning, April 18, 1974, I went to the bathroom and locked the door as I usually did. I rolled up some cotton on a toothpick to clean my ears. I put it into my ear to wipe off the pus that must have oozed overnight. However, the cotton on the toothpick was clean. I tried again, but nothing came out on it. 'What happened? Why is this clean?' I cleaned the other ear. No dirt or pus was on it. Suddenly my heart began to pound. I seemed to hear again the testimonies that the patients at the Hyun Shinae Prayer House made, 'The living God healed all my diseases!'

Trying to calm myself down, I looked at my hands to see if any pus was on my fingers. 'Uh, where's the pus gone? No pus! Wow! It's dried!' I could see no yellow pus. Only black scabs formed over that special night. I rolled up my sleeves to check my elbows. Just black scabs were there. I could not stay in the bathroom any more. I rushed into the room and took off my clothes. Right before I checked my knuckles and bones, my heart raced with curiosity. No pus remained on my knees and ankles.

With my eyes wide open I checked my neck with my fingers. I felt no mass there. 'Where have the grape-size masses gone? They were here. Where are they? They've disappeared! No more mass in my neck!' I touched and rubbed all over my neck, but I could not feel any mass. Everything was surprising me. I felt somewhat lost. My heart beat too loudly and my breath almost stopped.

I held my head in both my hands and leaned against the wall. I went back to my memory... How was I the morning before? I could not get up when I first woke up. I had to sit against the wall for a while before I stood up to go to bathroom, almost crawling.

How was I this morning? I got up easily... felt no dizziness... and no pain when I walked... I straightened my knees. It was easy for me. I felt no pain. I bent my knees. No pain again.

God healed me!

How could this be? I didn't take any medicine or shot. How could I have gotten this miracle? God must have healed me! Trying to calm myself down, I thought over what happened at the Hyun Shinae Prayer House when my sister and I went.

I walked up to the 3rd floor with great effort... my body became hot like fire when I knelt down to pray... then my fear disappeared... it was easy for me to walk down after I received the prayer... I wondered why... since then I could walk... all my diseases were healed there! I was healed and was able to walk and hear! Oozing from the sores stopped so that my skin dried! The masses in my neck were melted away! Yes! Yes!

I nodded to myself, and I had to recognize that the living God produced this miracle in me. I could not help kneeling down before the almighty God. I did not know my tears were streaming down my cheeks.

"Oh, God! God! God! You are really living! You really healed me! How could You cure me this neatly? How could You get rid of all my diseases at once? I didn't believe that You are alive. I didn't believe that You could heal any fatal disease! I didn't believe in You before!"

I cried my heart out. Kneeling on the floor, looking up at the ceiling, I cried all my heart out, beating the floor and my chest.

"Oh, God! Thank You, God! Please forgive me, God! I used to say, 'Show me God, if He exists.' Please forgive me. God, thank You for healing me, one who was close to death. Thank You so much, God!"

My wife ran into the room on hearing my crying. "What's wrong with you, honey?" Seeing my clothes spread over the floor, she looked at me with concerned eyes.

"Honey! I got saved! Look at me! God healed me! God did!"

Oh, God! You are really alive!

She examined me, while I was stunned, from head to toe. She trusted what I said; "God healed me."

"Yes, honey! He is really living! He is really alive! And God is the Healer! This is a miracle! You can live a worthwhile life from now. I'm so happy for you, honey."

She was crying and talking to me with the happiest face I had ever seen.

We heard someone knock on the door. My wife walked out to serve the customers. The visitor was my sister. I could hear my wife talk to her rapidly, like a machine gun.

"Dear sister-in-law, thank you so much! Miyoung's dad was thoroughly healed after he received the prayer yesterday! He walks well and hears well now! Do you hear me, sister-in-law? God healed him all over! That's because of your help. I'll earnestly go to church to believe in Jesus."

Her voice, talking without pause, was full of rejoicing.

This was the day for me, who had been dying, to have new life given. It was the first day and the happiest day for me; I met the living God.

God saw the faith of the people who made an opening in the roof above Jesus and, after digging through it, lowered the mat the paralyzed man (their friend) was lying on. That's why God forgave the paralyzed man's sins and healed him. God also saw the faith of my elder sister who had supplications and love for me. That's why He forgave my sins and healed me.

My elder sister had earnestly prayed for me with tears that I might guide our family to salvation. God answered her because she fasted, prayed for several late nights and supplicated for me, and because He knew my heart.

I did not look for God, but He came to see me first because He is love. He called me because he knew I would not turn away but would manage a lot of missionary works as a servant of God. I obeyed His call so that when I knelt down to pray at the Hyun Shinae Prayer House, He burnt my whole body with the Holy Spirit to heal me. By this miracle I was healed at once, met God, and began to live a reborn life.

My sister came into the room, being at a loss for words. She started to pray to God with tears.

"Oh, God! Our living God! You healed my brother. Thank You, Father. You blessed him to know You. Thank You so much! He is reborn now. Please guide him to be one of Your beloved children.

God, You made the dead rise. I give You all the glory.

In the name of Jesus Christ, I pray."

3
OH, GOD!

My new life

One morning I was reborn

What a surprise that was! I found myself healthy when I woke up in the morning. Deep in my heart I knew it could happen, but how amazed I was that a miracle happened to me!

'Oh, wonderful God!'

I, who hadn't believed that God exists, met the invisible but living God one day. I changed into a person who calls and praises God. I came to kneel down before God, who gave me a healthy new life when I was wandering in the valley of death. I became a man worthy of life, being able to hear any sound that people hear, eat all kinds of foods, and do any kind of work.

I wanted to do something from the very start. I wanted to go to church like the other believers. I looked around my residential area. I was surprised to see that there were many churches. I could not make up my mind which one I would go to.

"There's one right behind our house. Isn't it the nearest one of the best?" said my wife.

We decided to go to the church located very close to our house.

My first day to go to church

I counted every hour until Sunday came. Finally my family and I headed for the church with anticipation. My steps were full of joy and light like flying. To my eyes my family looked so happy as to have nothing lacking for a good life. My wife and I walked with linked arms, and my daughter took my hand, going toward the new life.

"Daddy, why do we go to church?" asked my daughter. She was so excited and curious because we all went out together.

"Sweetie, God made me healthy and made us happy. That's why we go to church to thank Him."

Entering the church building, my heart was too full for words.

'You saved me! Thank you, God!'

We received a kind and warm welcome. When I sat in a seat, I felt a sort of trembling.

"God, finally today we are here at church. I regret that we haven't come earlier. Why didn't I know that it was this happy?"

The praising sounded peaceful and gave me comfort. I felt that I was in my hometown. The pulpit and the big cross did not look strange to me. The flowers decorating the pulpit were in full bloom as if they would welcome me. The members stood all together to sing the hymn and read the response. They looked like well-trained soldiers. I tried to join the congregation, following their singing and reading as much as possible. I did not feel any embarrassment, though.

The entire congregation sat and someone made the representative prayer for the service. On hearing the prayer spoken loudly, my tears welled up in my eyes, streaming down my cheeks with gratitude.

The next order was the choir's anthem. They rose and sang with happiness and strength. Their praising was so impressive. It seemed to fill up the sky with deep emotion.

The pastor delivered a message, talking about the love and grace of the Lord. I could not understand his preaching completely, but I felt gratitude and joy. The pastor looked like a white light, which fearfully blazed upon us, my wife and me.

When we gave offerings during the singing, I thought my offering was too little. So I decided to give more next time.

This was the first time my wife and I attended a worship service together. Unknowingly, I shed tears until the end. I saw my wife try to wipe the tears from her face many times. When the service was over, I did not feel like going home. So I sat back and prayed to God.

I became a Christian who prays to God

"Oh, God! You are really alive. Here I came to church with my family to attend the worship service. I thought I learned enough. Please forgive my arrogance in ignoring You. Please help me, a newborn baby. I believe You, the Almighty, who cured all of my diseases, will guide me. Oh, living God! Please teach me how to live my new life in the future."

I was glad and felt peaceful and confident. Attending the worship service, we received overflowing joy and grace.

Since that day, my wife and I began looking forward to the Sundays yet to come. Every Sunday we closed our snack bar to go to church. It was always a great pleasure.

We really wanted to have our own Bible and hymnbook. To buy them we needed to save money for several weeks. We could not afford the best ones, but we cherished the Bible very much because the word of God was written in it.

Reading was my hobby. When I was sick, reading books was my only enjoyment. So I began to read the Bible as soon as I bought it. I read it all day long without getting bored. The more I got to know of Jesus, the more I felt sorry for my foolishness. I was thankful and amazed at the power of God.

I acquired a habit to praise and pray at night.

Amazing grace! How sweet the sound!
That saved a wretch like me!

I once was lost, but now am found;
Was blind, but now I see.
'Twas grace that taught my heart to fear,
And grace my fears relieved.
How precious did that grace appear
The hour I first believed!

When I sang hymns, my tears welled up, my heart became full of joy, and almost automatically I raised my hands. Sometimes I imagined Jesus standing before me.

"Oh, Jesus! I have acted as if I knew everything, even God. I ignored my sister who tried to preach the gospel to me. And I yelled at her, 'Where's your living God?'

Sometimes I scorned those who earnestly praised and prayed, critically saying, 'They are crazy.' I disliked those who cried while praying. I asked myself, 'Why do they wail like that?'

Oh, Lord! I didn't trust Senior Deaconess Hyun, because she didn't pray for me in the way I expected. I didn't believe that those testimonies about God healing them were true. Please forgive me for being ignorant, foolish and arrogant.

Oh, my Lord, Jesus! You delivered me from death and gave me new life. You delivered me from sorrow and gave me rejoicing. You delivered me out of illness and gave me health! I cannot begin to describe with words how thankful I am.

Oh, God! You are God of love. You are God of wondrous power. I give all glory to You!

My Lord, how can I pay You back for Your grace? I have no money. With what can I pay you back, Lord? As I don't have anything but my body, I want to give You my heart, the most precious thing in me. Please accept my heart, thanking You beyond my descriptions."

I praised and prayed, being unaware of the passage of time.

I can do something!

When I realized that my seven years of illness, spent mostly in bed, was over, I had the hope to live a worthy life. I wanted to do something for my wife and children as the head of my family. Also I wanted to pay back God who gave me health as much as I could.

I had nothing but debts piled a mile high. However, I was confident of doing anything, without fear, because I believed in God who healed me.

Opening a business looked like the best way for me to pay off my debts. But I had no funds for that. We had borrowed money from every person we could. I really did not want to go ask for aid from my unbelieving brothers.

At that time, in 1974, I needed 40,000 Won (US $33) to pay just the monthly bills alone. So I could not get a job at 20,000 Won (US $17) a month. My new policy was that I must go to church on Sundays because I received blessings from God. So I did not get any big-paying job unless I got off on Sundays. It was very hard for me to find a good job. I really wanted to work, but I could not get what I thought was an adequate job.

One day a construction worker, one of my acquaintances, recommended we work together. I did not say yes because I had never worked in that field. He said, "Don't worry. I'll be with you."

I had to make a decision. 'The living God healed me at once. To repay God for His grace I must keep the Lord's Day. God will give me the financial blessing also. Until that time I'll do any work, even the heavy labor job. He gifted me with health. Why don't I work, then?'

With this strong will I went out to do this laborious job. No matter how hard I worked for myself, I could not finish more than half the work the others did. Feeling sorry, I wanted to quit. But I encouraged myself, 'Come on, Jaerock. If you can't do this, you can do nothing else.'

Although I suffered from tiredness every night, I punctually got up the next morning to go to work.

My sweet home

My wife was pleased with my new attitude, but she was also concerned about my working at a heavy labor job. I could see she was happy that I was working for the family after being sick for so long. My daughters, as other children did, waited for and welcomed me when I came back from work, hanging around my neck.

I felt love in my home for the first time in many years. I was happy for my family. They were so lovely and made my home sweeter and sweeter. Every day was new to us. As the bright sun rises, a bright promising future was rising with happiness for my family. My wife and I often praised God who gave us new life:

Lately the life of Christ burst out alive in me!
Old things have passed away, even myself is new.
His life floods through me, like rivers toward the sea,
His love shines on me like sun shining on the dew.
With Christ I'll savor life unending ev'ry day;
Now and forever I'll walk with Him all the way.

Please help me to forgive the others

When we went to my hometown

On July 10, 1974 my family planned to go down to my hometown to join my father's birthday party.

My home had no more fighting or pains, only love and peace. It was the first time for us to cultivate a happy and hopeful life since we got married.

I thought of my family members who had ignored me when I was sick. At first I was not willing to go see them. However, I made up my mind to forget the painful past so that I would go with peace in my heart, because God blessed me to regain my health. I even felt happy to have the opportunity in front of them to boast of God who healed and gave me a new life.

It has been a long time since I have been able to make a trip in a state of health and joy. The mountains, trees and everything passing by the train windows looked wonderful.

All of my family members gathered there. My father and

mother, brothers and their wives, sisters and their husbands, nephews and nieces... We were a big family. I enjoyed the party, serving the elderly guests for my father. My family members and villagers were surprised to see me healthy.

"This is a miracle, a miracle! You are blessed. Is it true that God cured you? I can't believe that. You were lucky. That's it."

Although they passed me congratulatory comments, they wouldn't try to believe that God cured me. Only my mother, when she began her Christian life and removed all idols from her house including Buddha's statue, would testify that God is living.

"How come you don't believe that God cured Jaerock? Don't you remember that I had prayed to many gods for many years and received nothing? But right after he and his sister went to pray to God, he came back thoroughly healed. You should believe that God really cured Jaerock who was dying. Only God can do that, only God!"

My parents must have been satisfied to see their sons and daughters enjoying themselves, because they had not had this type of enjoyment for a long while. My restored health just added another pleasure to the celebration.

My wife ran out of my home

When my wife was packing her belongings near the end of the party, my mother called her. My mother might have been feeling sorry that she said to me one year ago, 'You'd better die.'

"My dear daughter-in-law, you have gone through so much suffering. It must be your destiny to get your husband sick. Now he has become healthy. So please regard that as your bad luck. Forget the past and live a happy life from now on."

This statement made my wife's face turn deathly pale. She trembled and was struck dumb by shock.

"You mean, my husband got sick because of me?" My hot-tempered wife, at a loss for words, stood up abruptly.

"OK, then. I'll get a divorce, all right?" She shouted and rushed out.

My elder sister tried to stop her, "Hold on, sister-in-law. You are misunderstanding!" She shook off my sister's hand and ran out of the house.

I, drinking with my father and brothers, heard that my wife ran out.

"Mother, why did you say that? Couldn't you recognize her hard life instead? Why did you tell her I got sick because of her destiny?" Although I knew my mother was weak-minded, I could not hold my anger toward her.

I thought my wife would come back soon, after she had a break, because she left all of her belongings behind. But she did not come back, and I started to worry about her.

"How dare she go far away? She'll be back soon. Let's just talk while we wait for her."

"You know, brother. Your wife was too stubborn and wasteful. That's why you are poor now. Why don't you fix her attitude this time? What daughter-in-law dare get mad at mother-in-law and run out? It's not acceptable!"

My brothers tried to comfort me, but I did not like them speaking ill of my wife.

'Oh, my! What's wrong with this? I've just got my sweet home.'

I could not keep waiting for my wife any longer. All of my dreams seemed to be shattered. I felt so upset that I could not control myself. I ran into the kitchen, picked up a 750-ml bottle of Soju (a kind of cheap Korean whisky) and poured it into my mouth. I spoke to my brothers and parents in a loud drunken voice, expressing my complaints:

"Why do you talk badly of her behind her back? Do you think I like it? No way! I'm going to kill myself!"

My family members, who had been enjoying the party, were shocked at my frantic behavior. And guests started to gossip about my wife's running out and my threat of suicide. I was so embarrassed that I went to my sister's house to hide myself.

I understood my wife. She must have felt hurt by the way my mother mistreated her. She received no recognition of her suffering from my mother for taking care of me, her sick husband for that long seven years. I could understand why she ran out.

I did not want to keep waiting for her to show up. She just disappeared, leaving no signs I could follow. I assumed that my wife was so angry that she would go back to Seoul right away. I left my hometown for Seoul to find my wife. I took only my first daughter, Miyoung, with me. We caught a train, which ran too slowly to me. I was sorry that I had no other way to go faster to Seoul. My mind was full of seeing my wife as soon as possible.

Arriving home in Seoul, I called to my wife in a loud voice. "Honey, open the door! We're home!"

I thought my wife would come out to greet us. But no signs of her were seen. We rushed to the snack bar. It was locked. I did not have any strength to walk. I felt that I lost everything.

My sweet home was shattered

My worry started to grow. I could not give up my sweet home, because I had not felt happy for a long time.

She left nothing behind her for us - her husband and two daughters. I searched for her, asking around, but I could not find her.

On the next day she returned home. She looked too different from what she had been. I had doubted that she would get a divorce. I was wrong. My hope was shattered.

"I'm leaving you, OK? I have already filed for divorce in my hometown, Mokpo."

My wife looked firmly determined. I was struck dumb with disappointment. I could not say even a word to her.

One day later, my wife came with her brothers and sisters to take everything that she brought with her when we got married.

"She's not your wife any more! Don't try to stop us."

They took out everything. They emptied my house, leaving us a cold wind. I really did not want to see them doing that.

They even tried to get the rental contract deposit money refunded.

My five-year-old daughter, Miyoung, was crying, holding my wife's skirt. "Mommy, don't go! Stay with us, please!"

"You have to keep your determination. No pity at all! Don't look behind you."

My wife, hesitating a little between her families and her daughter, pushed away her daughter. Miyoung rushed to cling to her mother's skirt. She begged again, "Mommy, don't go, please. No, no!"

But my wife left us, never looking back. They disappeared by truck right in front of us. There was no pity left at all behind them.

Miyoung, being unaware of her shoes coming off, tried to stop her mother again. Her crying, following her mother and rolling her body on the ground did not make any change on my wife. Miyoung, stopping her crying, showed her seriousness and said to me, "Daddy, she's not my mommy any more. I'm not going to call her 'Mommy' from now on."

I was shocked to hear that. She was too young to say this. It was making another hole of loneliness and sadness in my heart.

I encouraged myself, still hoping that my wife would not file a divorce. As of that date I began to pray.

"God, my wife left our home. Please send her back to me so that we may get our sweet home back and cultivate good faith, and so she may take good care of our children. I believe You will help me."

I earnestly prayed for fifteen days. And during those fifteen days I checked possible relatives' houses where my wife might have stayed.

"She's not your wife any more, is she? Give her up. It won't be possible to find her. Why don't you try to find another woman to marry?"

My mother-in-law never allowed me to step into her house. I was terribly hurt that all of my wife's family supported her in getting divorced.

After my wife ran out, I sent my daughter, Miyoung, to my parents who were living in the countryside.

One day an emergency call from the countryside came to me. It was about my daughter, Miyoung, who was hospitalized because she suffered from a malignant skin disease.

My parents said, "Miyoung is in coma at the hospital now. She intermittently kept calling 'Mommy.' You'd better find her mother and bring her to see Miyoung; it may be the last time."

I forcefully headed to my wife's parents'. My mother-in-law responded to my request. "Isn't it better for both of you? You and my daughter don't have to feel sorry for her any more, if she dies... It might make it easier for you to remarry."

Even though Miyoung could not see her mother, she still survived. I couldn't take it any more. I became exhausted and terribly disappointed by the vicious attitude of people. I walked into a bad world.

I met God, and I knew how to pray. But I did not know the word of God. So I did not have any strength to fight against the pain of misfortune that suddenly hit me like a cyclonic wind.

I drank over and over until I lost myself. I hated my mother who caused our divorce. I hated my wife who got mad at a misunderstanding and filed for a divorce. I hated my wife's family who never allowed me to come see my wife. I drank to forget the people I hated.

I smoked myself sick. My poor daughters... I smoked not to think of my two daughters abandoned by their parents who were still alive. I blew smoke-rings together with the faces of my daughters into the air. As the smoke-rings faded away, simultaneously my sorrow for my daughters faded away.

Whenever I got money, I spent it for pleasure to forget everything.

I regained the strength, relying on only Jesus

Some days later I began to feel heavy in my heart.

When I cried out, "I cannot lose the happiness I just found," God gave me this instructive message:

'Who gave you your health back? It was God. Who can save you from the pain now? Only God can. Wasting time by straying from the right path cannot bring any solution. Your happiness has already gone. You have no way to bring it back now. Leave everything to God, and rely on Him.'

I had to admit that my marriage broke down.

Marriage, according to Genesis 2:24, means that a man leaves his father and mother and is united with his wife, and becomes one flesh.

If a spouse leaves home when he or she does not get along with the other, automatically their marriage breaks down. I suffered from the breakdown of my marriage, which was caused by my wife. But I never forgot God.

I could regain my strength, relying on Jesus.

Out of my bondage, sorrow and night,
Jesus I come, Jesus I come;
Out of my shameful failure and loss,
Jesus I come, Jesus I come.
Into The glorious gain of Thy cross,
Jesus, I come to Thee.
Out of earth's sorrows into Thy balm,
Out of life's storms into Thy calm,
Out of distress to jubilant psalm,
Jesus I come to Thee.
Out of myself to dwell in Thy love,
Out of despair into raptures above,
Upward for aye on wings like a dove,
Jesus I come to Thee.

My wife united and became one flesh with me. We shared all of the suffering together and accepted Jesus at the same time. However, when she abandoned me, I realized the truth: Only God will not abandon me at any time, in any circumstance.

My wife and I were separated. She finally got a divorce just as she used to say to me during my illness, "I'll get a divorce, once you get well."

As written in Proverbs 13:2-3, *'From the fruit of a man's mouth he enjoys good, but the desire of the treacherous is violence. The one who guards his mouth preserves his life; the one who opens wide his lips comes to ruin.'* my wife's complaint came true. Exactly as she mentioned, we got divorced. How fearful it is!

Our divorce caused my father to get sick. My mother urged me to remarry whenever she saw me. Of course every time I objected:

"Mother, I can't think of living with any one else except for Miyoung's mom. She will come back to me for sure."

Since I decided to leave everything to God, I tried to abolish the affection remaining in my heart for my wife.

One day I went out to meet a lady, because my mother forced me. My mother said that the lady was a warm-hearted woman and always nice to her parents.

At the meeting place I saw the lady. She was the ideal woman I had always dreamed. It was unbelievable to me to meet the kind of woman I had dreamed about. We found that we liked each other. So, both our parents started to prepare for our marriage.

Some days later, my wife showed up unexpectedly. She said she had something to confess to me. She threw herself into my arms and burst into tears.

"I was wrong, honey. I was so bad to you. Please forgive me."

I had already decided to forget my wife and to remarry. No spousal affection could stay in my heart, because her abandoning our daughters and me had caused such a dreadful disappointment. If anything remained in my heart, it was hatred for her.

If God were in my situation, what would He do? I prayed for His advice.

"God, my wife is back and asking me to forgive her. Jesus said, 'Forgive not up to seven times, but up to seventy times seven.' Thinking of my painful life after she ran out, I still have some hatred in me. Father, what should I do? I have even promised to marry another woman soon. Is this lady better than my wife to raise my daughters who are still young? Please tell me what I should do, God."

I told my wife, "You'd better go back. Although I forgive you, my family won't forgive you."

She did not back down. Her attitude was firmly determined. "I'll get forgiveness from everybody. I belong to you and your family. I won't leave this house."

My wife was normally a meek woman, but she looked absolutely different.

I told her I could forgive her with the following conditions:
She must obey me, her husband, 100%. She should go get forgiveness from my parents and all of my family members. Her family has to come and apologize to me. She promised she would do everything.

I went to the mother of the woman I would marry. She

complained to me. "Why did you cancel the wedding? Have you found any problem with my daughter? If not, you can't do this!"

I explained to her the story in detail. Unexpectedly she agreed with the cancellation.

My wife came back to me

Consequently I forgave my wife and reunited with her. It had been 120 days since she left me. During those days God changed my stubborn wife to become submissive, like a sheep.

Later I realized that this was part of God's work in my family.

At the beginning of November when the fall season reached its peak, my wife brought everything of hers back home. We started to rebuild our happy nest, our sweet home.

Although the breakdown of my marriage hurt me, I never missed attending church because I had believed in the living God. Attending church, however, did not give me the full understanding of the word of God.

One day my new landlord encouraged me to participate in the revival at Sungdong Church located in Oksoo-dong. With new resolution my wife and I earnestly participated in every meeting of the revival, from dawn to night. Every time we prepared an offering for God and we took the best seats in the front to receive the abundant grace God would give us.

My wife made a crying repentance when she listened to the sermon about Ruth, who was widowed but served her mother-in-law, Naomi, very well. My wife, who had been mad at her mother-in-law, repented. She also repented for running away and getting a divorce.

"Mother-in-law, I was a bad daughter-in-law. From now on I'll do my best, serving you, just as Ruth did for Naomi."

I was happy to see my wife changed. Before, she had made an involuntary apology to my mother so that we could recover our marriage and cancel my wedding plans with another single woman.

I also received the overflowing grace of God. I quit drinking and smoking. I learned what and how I should live as a Christian who really loves God. As of that date, I added this topic to my prayer: "God, please help me to get rid of evil in my heart."

Please help me to forgive the others

"Everyone who hates his brother is a murderer; and you know that no murderer has eternal life abiding in him" (1 John 3:15).

"Anyone who does not practice righteousness is not of God, nor the one who does not love his brother" (1 John 3:10).

The pastor's preaching touched me on the sore part of my heart. I prayed with all my heart.

"Oh, Lord! I remember my mother-in-law, who called me, 'Cripple', 'Liar.' Please help me to forget that bad memory of her.

Jesus! Please melt my hatred for my wife, who complained to me for making no money. Please forgive me who told my wife, 'I'll get my revenge on you when I am rich after I recover my health.'

Oh, Lord! I still remember that my parents and brothers abandoned and abused me, saying, 'You'd better die.' Please make my hatred melt away so that I may forgive them.

Jesus! I hated those who judged me by my appearance not by my heart, ignoring me with my inability to make money. They compliment those who they like, but ignore or abuse those who they dislike. Please help me to feel love instead of hatred for those people.

Please help me to forgive everybody."

My wife and I cried at every meeting in the revival. We cried for our sorrowful days of the past. We cried and were thankful for the love of God, who made us able to forgive everybody.

Oh, God! You changed my hatred to love!
You reformed my hatred into forgiveness!
You changed my misfortune to happiness!
Thank You for Your majesty!

God worked on my family and me. He changed the stormy things - my wife's running out, divorce and reunion - to a peaceful life of obedience and love.

Until the end of my journey

After the cyclone passes, it becomes quiet. Likewise, after my wife came back, my home settled down.

My wife, who wanted to be forgiven by my family, made her resolution to live a new life. My family was very pleased with her change. I also wanted to live a worthwhile and happy life with my forgiven wife.

I seemed to have nothing to envy, if I lived by the grace and love of God who healed me at once. The happiest thing for us was that we would live in joy and peace in this world and then go to heaven. How wonderful heaven will be! There is no tears, sorrow, pain or disease in heaven. We will live there forever by the love of God.

I liked it because there is no disease there and because I had already suffered from diseases. I really believed in heaven and wished to go there because I was ignored and despised by many people, shedding tears and chewing sorrow in this world.

Deciding to live my life as a child of God, I asked Almighty God to take care of everything of mine so that I might live under His protection and guidance.

"Oh, Heavenly Father! You are my real Father. I am Your son. I want to live my life as Your child. Please always watch me, guide me, teach me and help me. You are my Father forever in this world and in heaven."

I wanted to love God

One day God gave me a wonderful blessing through the message of a sermon. *"I love those who love me; and those who diligently seek me will find me"* (Proverbs 8:17). I couldn't understand exactly what it meant, but I eagerly wanted to love God and be loved by Him. I really wanted to seek and find Him.

From this date my life became absolutely renewed.

I never missed a worship service. On Sunday morning, Sunday evening and Wednesday evening I loved God by attending all of the services. Once I heard the message, I did my best to practice just what was said.

I could not understand all of the messages delivered in the services. I did not have any counselor for my faith to grow. Although I could not completely understand the word of God by myself, I did my best to follow His teachings.

'In everything give thanks.' I kept this message in my heart. I searched myself to see if I gave thanks in everything. As I checked myself, I had given thanks in all of my circumstances.

"God, I thought I had given thanks in everything. But I remember that I didn't give thanks for my heavy labor job before. I don't think You would say that I gave thanks in all circumstances. Please help me to give thanks in everything from now on."

I prayed to God like a child, talking with Him. Then God let me know whether or not I gave thanks. This was God's way to teach me why I should give thanks.

I still worked in construction sites. I had to get up early in the morning to go to work. My job was a very difficult one. So, during my sleep at night I groaned, and my whole body ached.

My mind kept saying to me, 'Quit.' But I encouraged myself to overcome it. As time passed, I felt less tired. My appetite became stronger and I came to eat more. Whatever I ate, I digested very well. I felt confident in doing any hard job. My body became healthier and stronger.

God let me take this laborious job. I thanked God for His wisdom and love. "Oh, God! Thank You so much! You made me labor and work. How could I know that it's Your way? I understand now. I realized how wise You are and how wonderful Your love is."

Although I was cured, my body was not strong yet because I had not exercised for a long time. To make my body stronger, God gave me difficult works to do. I deeply thanked God for this.

Since I practiced the biblical messages in my daily life, God guided me to live as one of His children.

Some nights I could not fall asleep. Instead of sleeping, I enjoyed dreaming of my future, how I would cultivate my new life, living as a child of God.

My sweet home

My biggest hope was to live by the word of God and to make my sweet home. I prayed to Almighty God. I knelt down and prayed to God because I believed that He would answer me for sure.

"Oh, heavenly Father! You are our Guide! Thank You for giving my family joy and life. Thank You for giving us faith. Father, please bless me to cultivate my faith more preciously during my life in this world. Please bless me to have better hope. Please bless me to have more precious love.

Before I accepted Jesus, I had no faith, only pain. I had no hope, only sorrow. I had no love, only grief. But now I do love our Lord."

I kept praying.

"Please bless me to love my wife more, bless my wife to serve me well, and bless us to take care of our children well so that we may build a sweet home. Please guide me to live a happy life with faith to the end of my journey. Please help me to live a joyful life with hope. Please bless me to live a peaceful life with love."

I earnestly prayed. I believed that God would not allow any shadow of misfortune to come to my family again.

My family made a sweet home as we prayed, overflowing with rejoicing and thanksgiving, with love and peace, and with praising and praying. If there was anything we were in need of, it was money. After my wife ran out to file for divorce, her snack bar was shut. Automatically the interest on the debt increased, which made our finance worse.

My policy was that I had to pay back my creditors although I had no food to eat. I worked harder. I did any dirty or heavy job, whatever came to me. I did many kinds of laborious work.

My wife also worked very hard. She sometimes bought salted clams in Inchon at wholesale price to make a profit, handled brown seaweeds, and worked a job carrying rocks. Both of us worked really hard to earn money. We felt no shame in any job, only joy.

I wanted to glorify God

I had another wish. As one of the children of God, I wanted to be blessed at my God-given-work and to glorify Him, helping the poor people. In my prayer I believed that He would bless me with a new better job.

"God, You gave me health. I believe You will give me blessings too. Doing some laborious works, I've waited for a good job You would give me. God, please give a great job to me very soon. You know everything about my financial situation. I believe You will bless me with a wonderful job."

I prayed for financial blessing because I desired to fulfill my duty as the head of my family and to serve the kingdom of God. My desire, to be an elder and then work for the church, was getting stronger. Although I was in need of several things, I did not ask anyone for help. I thought it would not glorify God, if I received a help from other people. When my second brother volunteered to support me, I rejected it. That's because if I become prosperous in the future through his support, the glory would not go to God but to him.

Another good-paying job was offered to me. I immediately rejected it, because they wanted me to work two Sundays a month. I would not break the Lord's Day for money. I would not accept any job offer with a big salary, if it caused me to violate God's decrees. I just waited for the day God would open the door to blessings for me. I willingly kept on doing laborious jobs.

I wanted to spread the gospel

I had a third wish.

"God, You completely healed me of all my diseases. I believe that You will protect my family and me from any disease. When I was healed, it was the first time for me to meet You and believe in You, The Living God. There are so many sick people in this world. I'd like to let them know You are the living God."

I tried to spread the gospel to as many people as possible. I earnestly talked to them about how God healed me, how many diseases I had had before I was cured, how much God loved us, and what blessings we would get when we believed in Jesus Christ. I talked about God and His healing to my fellow laborers, relatives and neighbors.

My family had nothing to boast of in the sight of the others. But we were rejoicing all the time and giving thanks in everything. Not only I, but also my wife and children had no other business that made us feel happier than going to church.

Always praising songs flowed from my house. My kids danced and sang quite often. They were cute and wonderful to see. I could tell how happy our God would feel to see them.

My family had been under pain without knowing God.

After we knew God we became happy, receiving the love of God. Since then, we put our hope in heaven so that we came not to envy wealth and honor in this world.

When we went to church with new neighbors, we walked more happily than the other days. Spontaneously I sang out in praise, and my wife joined my singing.

> All the way my Savior leads me;
> What have I to ask beside?
> Can I doubt His tender mercy,
> Who thro' life has been my guide?
> Heav'nly peace, divinest comfort,
> Here by faith in Him to dwell;
> For I know whate'er befall me,
> Jesus doeth all things well.
> For I know whate'er befall me,
> Jesus doeth all things well.

4

CHARACTER PRODUCES HOPE

I was a sinner

My wife and I were living a new life with new hope. One day God gave us a big blessing.

It was in November 1974, when Oksoo-dong Sungdong Church was holding a revival. In the revival, the main speaker Rev. Byong-ok Pak was preaching under the topic, 'Let's give out everything we have!'

In the evening meeting on Monday, the speaker Rev. Pak came down from the altar and laid his hands on my wife and me. It was an unexpected special prayer for us.

On the next day we couldn't attend the morning meeting for some reasons. Later we heard that the speaker looked for us when we were absent and he said, "God prepared this revival for a certain couple that are absent now. They should not miss any meeting. Please let them know, if you live near to them." After hearing that, we attended all of the services and meetings from Tuesday evening.

Through the speaker's preaching I learned that God created everything in the universe and mankind, and He sent His only Son Jesus to redeem us from our sins. I could feel His love and existence in my heart.

We should believe in God the Creator

To believe in Jesus, we must start with the recognition 'I am a sinner.' If I do not recognize that I am a sinner, I cannot believe that Jesus died on the cross to redeem us from sin.

It is written in Matthew 1:21, *"She will bear a Son; and you shall call His name Jesus, for He will save His people from their sins."*

To admit that we are sinners, we must believe that God created all creatures including mankind and has controlled everything for us - birth, death, misfortune and fortune.

As God stated in Genesis 1:1, at the very beginning of the Bible, *"In the beginning God created the heavens and the earth."* He created day and night, sky and ground, sea, plants, sun, moon, stars, animals and man.

"Then the LORD God formed man of dust from the ground, and breathed into his nostrils the breath of life; and man became a living being" (Genesis 2:7).

"God created man in His own image, in the image of God He created him; male and female He created them. God blessed them; and God said to them, 'Be fruitful and multiply, and fill the earth, and subdue it '"

(Genesis 1:27-28) .

This is the account of the Creation: God the Creator planned, created and has governed everything.

On the other hand, there is the doctrine of evolution. The doctrine of evolution says that life was formed accidentally and it developed into each kind independently. Some evolutionists are, however, currently disregarding this doctrine.

It is true that how we live our lives is up to what doctrine we believe in. Those who put the origin of life in evolutionism will live for earthly desires, based on humanism. Oppositely, those who believe that God created everything will live according to the will of God the Creator, based on heavenly desires.

Which doctrine should we believe in?

Let's look at a high-rise building. First, the architect designs the building with his wisdom, as he wants. Construction workers build it from the ground as designed. No building can be built without a plan. TV sets or radios cannot be produced without a plan, either.

What about the solar system, which runs without making even the slightest error? What about all the other things in the universe that are moving in order and harmony? Nothing was made coincidentally. God planned and created every single item of the universe. We must believe this is true.

How was man created?

God formed man from the dust of the ground in His own image. He made a man with good care and love as the potter makes a pot. When He breathed the breath of life into his nostrils, the man became a living being. The man came to breathe and have blood circulating in his body. God also gave him a heart and mind with which he can move and think as a living being. Likewise, when we supply the electricity to the TV set we make, the TV shows us pictures and sounds.

If a man can make machines like this, the almighty God should know how to create man who thinks, speaks and moves.

God walked with Adam, the first man He created, and taught him about the harmony of the universe, the laws of the spiritual realm, and the words of truth.

"Be fruitful and multiply, and fill the earth, and subdue it; and rule over the fish of the sea and over the birds of the sky and over every living thing that moves on the earth" (Genesis 1:28).

"From any tree of the garden you may eat freely; but from the tree of the knowledge of good and evil you shall not eat, for in the day that you eat from it you will surely die" (Genesis 2:16-17).

"A man shall leave his father and his mother, and be joined to his wife; and they shall become one flesh"

(Genesis 2:24).

As above, God taught Adam step by step how he should live as the lord of all creation. God led him also to the path of blessing.

Why did God create man?

Although God had been with the heavenly hosts and angels, He created man. He knew beforehand that man would obey at first but eventually disobey Him. Why then did He create man?

Human beings know that they have to carry their babies for 9 months until they give birth. They know well that it will be very painful when they deliver a baby. They also know that they have to go through troubles to raise their children. Why then do parents want children? It's because they want to exchange love with their children.

Likewise, our Father God wanted to have His true children to exchange love with Him. The heavenly hosts and angels were like robots that did not have free will but obeyed only. That is why God created man who had thinking ability with free will. He wanted to exchange love with this man who had thinking ability.

God had set up the plan of 6,000 years' cultivation of the human being to raise His true children to live in truth. These 6,000 years are the human history since Adam and Eve were driven out of Eden due to their disobedience. It is described in detail in the Bible.

Why did Adam and Eve disobey God?

God taught Adam and Eve the good only, none of the evil. Adam had lived with all kinds of animals in the Garden of Eden where there was no evil, walking together with God for countlessly long time. For those innumerable years Adam had lived a happy life, being fruitful and increasing in number.

While Adam lived with God, Satan was searching for a way to tempt Adam to betray God. Adam and Eve were always under the deep love of God. So Satan, who had been searching any possible way of temptation, chose the serpent, more crafty than any of the wild animals.

In Genesis 3, knowing well the will of God, the serpent yielded to Satan because of its craftiness.

The serpent asked Eve, *"Indeed, has God said, 'You shall not eat from any tree of the garden'?"* (v. 1)

She replied to the serpent, *"From the fruit of the trees of the garden we may eat; but from the fruit of the tree which is in the middle of the garden, God has said, 'You shall not eat from it or touch it, or you will die'"* (vv. 2-3).

Satan saw that his temptation worked on Eve to change God's word from 'You will surely die' to 'You will die.' So Satan tempted Eve more intensely, directly opposing the word of God.

"You surely will not die! For God knows that in the day you eat from it your eyes will be opened, and you will be like God, knowing good and evil" (vv. 4-5).

Eve did not fight against Satan with the word of God, but replied with some doubt of it. Therefore Satan was able to put into Eve the worldly desires—last of the flesh, lust of the eyes, and pride of life.

"When the woman saw that the tree was good for food, and that it was a delight to the eyes, and that the tree was desirable to make one wise, she took from its fruit and ate; and she gave also to her husband with her, and he ate" (v. 6).

From that moment, the tragic history of mankind began. Adam was given the authority to subdue the earth and rule over all creatures. However, he disobeyed the Sovereign God who taught him the law—fear God and do not eat the fruit from the tree of the knowledge of good and evil. This is the reason Adam and Eve became sinners.

God asked Adam, *"Have you eaten from the tree of which I commanded you not to eat?"* (Genesis 3:11)

So the Lord God banished Adam and Eve from the Garden of Eden because He had warned them, *"For in the day that you eat from it you will surely die"* (Genesis 2:17). After He drove them out, He placed guards on the way to the tree of life.

After all, their spirit died after they were driven out of the spiritual realm. Furthermore, a lot of pain and curses followed. To the woman, God greatly increased her pain in childbearing. So, it was painful for woman to give birth to children. Her desire became for her husband, and he came to rule over her. The man, only through painful toil, could survive all the days of his life. He was to eat the plants of the field, but only by the sweat of his brow could he eat his food. And he was destined to die, going back to dust.

The serpent was cursed above all the other animals. It came to crawl on its belly and eat dust all the days of its life. God said to the serpent, *"I will put enmity between you and the woman, and between your seed and her seed; He shall bruise you on the head, and you shall bruise him on the heel"* (Genesis 3:15).

Here, 'dust' spiritually means man made of dust. 'The serpent will eat dust' means that due to Adam's disobedience man came to be food for the serpent, that is, man came under the control of the enemy Satan.

Likewise, Adam's disobedience resulted in a big fall. Adam, who used to be the ruler over the earth, was cursed so that everything under his rule was also cursed. And all of his descendents were cursed to be sinners. They all became heirs of damnation, for the wages of sin is death. (Romans 3:23; 6:23)

Moreover, all of Adam's authority was handed over to Satan because of his disobedience. (Luke 4:6) So the world became full of pain, sorrow, diseases, fighting and wickedness.

How can we be saved?

Our Father God foreknew that Adam would disobey. But He did not want Adam, His child, to become a child of Satan. That is why God prepared the way to salvation for His children. The way to salvation is only through Jesus Christ.

"For God so loved the world, that He gave His only begotten Son, that whoever believes in Him shall not perish,

but have eternal life" (John 3:16).

"But as many as received Him, to them He gave the right to become children of God, even to those who believe in His name" (John 1:12).

All human beings are destined to die. That is why Jesus came to this world about 2,000 years ago. He was crucified as a ransom to take all our sins.

God had set the way to eternal life. If we believe in Jesus who was crucified and rose again, we get forgiveness and eternal life as the children of God. How wonderful and thankful this is! Our God has given us this type of love. Hallelujah!

I was reborn as a child of God by realizing that I was a sinner

Although God has loved us so much, we haven't realized that He created the universe for us and let us rule over it.

"Oh, heavenly Father! Everyone in my family was a sinner. We didn't know of You. We didn't recognize You, either. You sent Jesus to die on the cross for us. Thank You for forgiving us. You let us know you through Your miraculous healing. Thank You for Your grace"

My tears of gratitude were flowing down. If God had not given me grace, I would still be living a painful life as a sinner who does not know God and is destined to die. How abundantly God has given His love to me! He gave me His love for nothing! How wonderful and how thankful His love is!

God healed me before I accepted Jesus Christ. Why did He give me this privilege? It is because He knew that I would not forget His grace or leave Him, and because He listened to my elder sister's earnest prayers for me. That is why God healed me, answering my sister's prayers.

For these reasons, I made up my mind to return God's love and grace. So I earnestly attended worship services and practiced what the word of God said I have become a reborn man with a big change in my life, from being cursed to becoming blessed.

"Oh, Father! God of love! Thank You for curing me and letting me know the way to salvation and everlasting life. Thank You for blessing me to be Your child and destroying the sin in me. Please bless me that I may have everything anew and become a true child of Yours!"

The cross of the Lord

I could not count how many blessings I had received from God. I must have been the world record holder in the Guinness Book of Records.

All of my family accepted Jesus together. My wife became as meek as a sheep in four months and built our sweet home. I was healed of seven years' illness, so that I worked hard but joyfully with my recovered health. Whenever I thought of all these blessings, I gave glory to God, who produces hope through character.

As a child of God

I realized that I was a sinner. So I wanted to live as a true child of God. How can I live according to the word of God? To live by the word of God was my goal and duty. I was so hungry and thirsty for righteousness that I tried to attend as many revivals as possible. I wanted to appreciate the grace of God given through the messages. While reading the Bible, I had time to read it attentively, because every word was important in throwing away my evil ways. If I failed to throw away an evil habit or to do something the scripture taught me, I would fast to be guided by God.

When I could not fully understand any biblical phrases, I asked my pastor. He advised me to buy a bible commentary, but it did not satisfactorily answer all of my questions. I really wanted to understand the word of truth clearly. So I often went to prayer houses, where I fasted, attended overnight meetings and earnestly prayed to ask God.

"Father, please give me clear answers for my questions. I'm sorry that my pastor's answer doesn't clear my confusion, and commentary books show me too many different interpretations. I believe I can get the true answers if I am filled with the Holy Spirit. I even heard that an angel came down to someone to answer his biblical questions for three years. Father, would You please help me to fully understand Your Scriptures? Please answer my prayer in your way."

One day I was praising and praying inspirationally.

Walking in sunlight all of my journey,
Over the mountains, through the deep vale,
Jesus had said, 'I'll never forsake thee.'
Promise divine that never can fail.
Heavenly sunlight, heavenly sunlight,
Flooding my soul with glory divine:
Hallelujah! I am rejoicing
Singing His praises, Jesus is mine.

My wish was to walk in light. I was wondering what light is
and how I can walk in light. A biblical message came into my
mind.

*"In the beginning was the Word, and the Word was with
God, and the Word was God. He was in the beginning
with God. All things came into being through Him, and
apart from Him nothing came into being that has come
into being. In Him was life, and the life was the Light of
men. The Light shines in the darkness, and the darkness
did not comprehend it. There came a man sent from
God, whose name was John. He came as a witness, to
testify about the Light, so that all might believe through
him. He was not the Light, but he came to testify about
the Light. There was the true Light which, coming into
the world, enlightens every man. He was in the world,
and the world was made through Him, and the world
did not know Him. He came to His own, and those who
were His own did not receive Him. But as many as
received Him, to them He gave the right to become*

*children of God, even to those who believe in His name,
who were born, not of blood nor of the will of the flesh
nor of the will of man, but of God. And the Word
became flesh, and dwelt among us, and we saw His
glory, glory as of the only begotten from the Father, full
of grace and truth" (John 1:1-14).*

God began to inspirationally help me to realize why Jesus
came to the world.

Why did Jesus come to the world?

According to the rule of the spiritual realm, Adam and Eve
became children of Satan because they committed a sin. To
return to God as His children they should have no sin. So they
needed someone to atone for their sins. No one in the world
could do that. That is why Jesus came in the flesh from God to
be a ransom for us.

Jesus had no sin because He was conceived by the Holy
Spirit. He had power to overcome the devil because He is the
Son of God. Most importantly He had love and died on the
cross for us. He came to the world, healed the sick, forgave
sinners, restored the demon-possessed to health, and gave
people liberty, peace, joy and love.

Satan, however, left no means untried to eventually crucify
the righteous Jesus. Satan knew that the woman's offspring
would recover the authority, which was handed to him. So
Satan tried all means to get Jesus, King of kings, the offspring
of the woman, crucified. When he succeeded in executing

Jesus, he shouted with delight for his victory.

God's love

"We speak God's wisdom in a mystery, the hidden wisdom which God predestined before the ages to our glory; the wisdom which none of the rulers of this age has understood; for if they had understood it they would not have crucified the Lord of glory" (1 Corinthians 2:7-8).

The enemy Satan did not know this wise providence of God, so he let people kill Jesus to get victory over Jesus. But to kill sinless Jesus was totally against the law of the spiritual realm.

Jesus did not have the original sin because He was conceived by the Holy Spirit. Jesus did not commit any sins because He lived according to God's commandments. It means that He cannot be put to death for any reason. However, the enemy Satan violated God's law, instigating Pilate, the Roman governor, to crucify Jesus. Since then, Satan lost the authority to rule over people only if they believe in Jesus Christ.

By the love of Jesus who was crucified, those who believe in Jesus become the children of God, moving from the children of Satan. Therefore salvation can be made in the name of Jesus Christ only.

As God foretold, Jesus came to the world in the flesh. He was conceived by the Holy Spirit and born of the Virgin Mary. He obeyed all commandments completely. He showed true love, even sacrificing Himself to be crucified.

'Heavenly Father! Now I clearly understand that Jesus came to the world to open the way to salvation for us to be children of God, so that we would not belong to the devil. Thank You so much for Your wisdom, the secret which was hidden before time began, and your love.'

The cross of Jesus

"Father, please let me know clearly why Jesus had to be hung on a tree and go through all those sufferings."

"Christ redeemed us from the curse of the Law, having become a curse for us—for it is written, 'Cursed is everyone who hangs on a tree' in order that in Christ Jesus the blessing of Abraham might come to the Gentiles, so that we would receive the promise of the Spirit through faith" (Galatians 3:13-14).

I could obviously understand that Jesus was hung on a tree to become a curse for us. He redeemed us from the curse in order that the blessing given to Abraham—faith, health, long life, prosperity and children—might come to us through Him. He let us become righteous by faith and receive the Holy Spirit to live as children of God.

When Jesus' side was pierced with a spear on the cross, blood and water gushed out. This evidently proves that Jesus, the Word, became flesh (John 1:14) and came to this world. At the same time it proves that if we, as the same flesh of Jesus, cultivate the heart of Jesus, we can be like Jesus even though we have physical body. That is why Philippians 2:5 says, *"Have this attitude in yourselves which was also in Christ Jesus."*

Jesus was whipped and shed His blood. I wondered why God allowed it to happen.

"But He was pierced through for our transgressions, He was crushed for our iniquities; the chastening for our well-being fell upon Him, and by His scourging we are healed" (Isaiah 53:5).

Jesus wore the crown of thorns, and so He was pierced. Why? He was pierced for our transgressions that we make through our thoughts.

Jesus was nailed through His hands and feet. Why? He was crushed for our iniquities that we make with our hands and feet.

Jesus said in Matthew 5:30, *"If your right hand makes you stumble, cut it off and throw it from you; for it is better for you to lose one of the parts of your body, than for your whole body to go into hell."*

When Jesus was crucified about 2,000 years ago, He was punished for our sins. He redeemed us from all of the sins of our past, present and future. How great His love is!

Walking in the light

"Father, I have a question. You said, once we believe in the cross of Jesus Christ, we receive eternal life. Then how come we have no life in us unless we eat the flesh of the Son of Man and drink His blood?"

To accept Jesus Christ does not mean that we commit no sin anymore. Jesus is the way, the truth and the life. (John 14:6) Since we eat the flesh of Jesus Christ, the word of truth, and drink His blood, we can get rid of our sins by the power of God who helps us to live by His word of truth. This is what the Bible says in 1 John 1:7; *"If we walk in the Light as He Himself is in the Light, we have fellowship with one another, and the blood of Jesus His Son cleanses us from all sin."*

As Acts 3:19 says, *"Therefore repent and return, so that your sins may be wiped away, in order that times of refreshing may come from the presence of the Lord,"* we must repent with all our heart and must not commit sin. That is why Jesus said in Matthew 7:21, *"Not everyone who says to Me, 'Lord, Lord,' will enter the kingdom of heaven, but he who does the will of My Father who is in heaven will enter."*

My life began to change and renew day by day. I earnestly kept on reading the Bible and hearing the messages. Once I discovered any sin in me, I prayed to throw it away. More often I fasted and prayed overnight. God saw this heart and attitude of mine, and He helped me to live in the truth. So I spent every single day with joy, living my life anew.

My love, the cross of the Lord;
Mighty cross flowing with
Grace and wisdom of God.

My life, the cross of the Lord;
The cross of the precious blood
That reveals the love and suffering of Jesus.

My joy, the cross of the Lord;
The cross of secret
That's hiding my sins and faults.

The living God

"Not everyone who says to Me, 'Lord, Lord,' will enter the kingdom of heaven, but he who does the will of My Father who is in heaven will enter" (Matthew 7:21).

"Blessed is he who reads and those who hear the words of the prophecy, and heed the things which are written in it; for the time is near" (Revelation 1:3).

I became one who reads and hears the word of God, and who prays, saying to Jesus Christ, 'Lord, Lord!' Gradually I could understand the word of God very deeply. I understood why we can be saved and get the hope for the kingdom of heaven if we believe in Jesus Christ. I felt in my heart that the love of God is as measureless as it is broader than the sky and deeper than the ocean.

I became one who receives Jesus Christ and believes in His name. So God gave me the right to become His child. The living God never left me alone like an orphan but kept me safe from sinning, because I was born of Him. He also guided and watched me, so evil could not harm me.

God saved me from an accident

After I accepted Jesus Christ as my Savior, God guided me to get a laborer job as construction worker. I was not sure if I could do the work, because I had no experience in it. However, I willingly started to do that job, which allowed me to get off on Sundays for the Sabbath until God opened the door of blessing to me.

The work was a lot harder than I had expected. It was impossible for me to catch up with the others, although I worked with no break. Fortunately I had patience, and I worked hard. My patience was so steadfast that I could complete my portion of work eventually.

I had only been a Christian for two months. No one had ever taught me how to pray. If I could, it was to recite the Apostles' Creed and the Lord's Prayer.

One day I felt a strong urge in my heart. From the early morning I really wanted to pray to God. So I was repeatedly reciting until I arrived at my construction site.

It was in the morning. I was about to stand up with some long pipes on my shoulder. I felt something strike me on the back and I lost my consciousness. Later I heard that I was like a frog, knocked down on the ground with all four legs stretched widely out. I was hit by a car. As I came back to my senses, I found myself surrounded by people worriedly talking about me. I got up, dusting off my clothes, as if nothing happened to me.

The driver (from Seoul City Hall) who hit me on the back looked quite pale and scared. "Are you all right? I'll get you to the hospital now." "No, no, you don't have to. I'm okay."

He knew that he hit me pretty hard. So he did not believe that I was not injured at all. It was miraculous to him. "Are you sure you have no injury? I don't think so."

My fellow workers had my clothes taken off and examined all over my body, wondering why not. "You'd better go to hospital. You can't tell about your backbone now. You should've your spine X-rayed. You might get some serious aftereffects." "I'll be all right, because my God protected me."

Honestly I felt no pain. Only the part where I was hit was a little swollen. I did not even have a bruise. It was mysterious to me too.

"If you would, go home and rest." My leader pleaded with me. But I stayed there until I finished my work for the day. When I got back home, I felt a little uneasiness. I was unable to go to work the next day. But God kept me thoroughly okay.

My fellows talked about the possible aftereffects. It was just a baseless anxiety, which remained in my mind for some seconds.

The driver who hit me heard of my absence and came to see me with worry on his face. He was so relieved to see I had no injuries. He begged me to forgive him, intending to pay me as little compensation money as possible. I responded to him, "I don't need any money from you."

He said to me, 'Thank you' several times. Later I found an envelope he left behind. It contained 2,500 Won (US $ 3) for me. Three dollars of compensation! How mean he was!

I drank not to feel tired

I kept working in construction here and there. Since I had no special skill in the construction field, I had to work as a general laborer, assisting technicians. Sometimes I carried sand or concrete mixture with a bucket on my back. To go upstairs without handrails was so hard that my legs trembled with weakness. The other carriers looked like they were running when they passed by me. I clenched my teeth, trying to catch them up. It was so heavy to me. I didn't feel like working in the afternoon, because I was too dizzy and tired. However, I encouraged myself to endure. 'Come on. I must do this.'

I could not give up there. I made up my mind to work as hard as I could. Thankfully, lighter jobs - opening cement bags, examining concrete mixture with a stick - were assigned to me. I was glad that I did not quit then. Through this heavy laborious work, the living God blessed me to cultivate my endurance and experience Him as the living God.

His blessing was not limited to me. This incident happened while I worked at a waterworks office near Walker Hill Hotel. My job was moving the concrete by a handcart from the mixer truck to the underground foundation of the building. I needed to pass through the bumpy road that was under construction. When I tried to unload the concrete and pour it into the deep spot, my body would also fall in there because I was not skillful at this job, compared to the others. If I made the slightest mistake, I might have fallen into the deep hole together with the concrete I poured down.

On that evening I heard an announcement that we were going to work a late night. Suddenly I felt disappointedly exhausted. The others drank some alcohol to gain some strength, but I had no energy remaining. I was too tired to take even a step. My body was like a wad of cotton fully soaked in water.

I was hesitating to make up my mind. I decided to drink some for the purpose of gaining strength. I quit drinking since I had attended revivals before. I thought that to drink a little would be okay. As soon as I drank some, I could feel that I was gaining power.

I was on the way home after work. In the bus I had a sudden dizziness and a severe headache. It was not endurable at all. I got off the bus in the middle to breathe fresh air, but it did not make any difference.

I came to realize that God would not allow me to drink at all. I repented of my drinking with all my heart. It was almost midnight when I plodded my way home, deeply thinking this and that.

'How long have I to do this heavy laborious work? God will give me the blessing in His right time. Didn't He say that blessed is the one who endures?'

I won't drink any more

A few months later I moved to a construction site in Wooi-dong where we started to build a two-floored house. My job was to dig the ground, standing in a narrow passage. I had to work without a break because of the workload. It was really hard. If I missed my morning prayer for the day, the work was a lot heavier to me.

My co-workers suggested that I should drink to feel less tired. Whenever they had a break with alcohol, they asked me to join them. At last I failed to refuse their request to drink.

It happened right after I drank. When I swung a pick down to dig the ground I heard my pick hit something, like solid rock or metal, so that it sprang back and struck me on the forehead. Immediately I could figure out that this accident resulted from my drinking. So I started to pray to God, holding my forehead that was bleeding badly.

"Oh, Father! Please forgive me. I'll never drink again."

Right then, my forehead stopped bleeding. My co-workers told me to go to the hospital. Instead of going to the hospital, I took a short break and completed my work for the day. The living God is the Lord who disciplines those He loves, and He punishes everyone He accepts as a son to guide to righteousness (Hebrews 12:6).

I threw away the desire for wealth

My wife began a new job as a cosmetics saleswoman. She was in charge of a good area and made decent money, enabling us to ease our financial difficulties.

I wanted to glorify God with financial blessing. However, my desire for wealth was too excessive. I made a business plan to open a bar with the money my wife would earn, while I would take care of our living with my income. We worked hard for our dream.

We were positive that we would make lots of money if we managed a restaurant serving alcoholic drinks and food, since my wife had good experience handling fried foods. The success of my sister's two-story Japanese restaurant was encouraging to us.

God knew that we had a strong desire for money, but He gave us an instruction: Do not get drunk on wine. It was then that we realized He would not be pleased with our plan.

If I had a strong desire since I attended the revival, it was to give more offerings to God. One night in my dream a big sow was giving birth to ten baby pigs. A lot of Koreans said that a pig in the dream means good luck. So I was willing to buy a lottery ticket.

"Honey, let's buy a lottery ticket. If we pray and buy, it will win. Then we can pay back all of our debts, leaving some money for offering."

After we bought a lottery ticket, we prayed to win for a week. We believed that our ticket would win the prize. It won no prize, though. Here, God gave us another instruction that we were wrong.

I quit playing Hwatoo (a Korean card game)

I often played Hwatoo on my days off. I was kind of a good gambler at Hwatoo, because I had played it for several years while I was sick. However, I was not a good player any more. I did not know why I kept losing money. I continued to play in order to win my lost money back.

One day I went to Boochun City, where I worked for several weeks. On the day when we got paid, we did not miss playing Hwatoo. It was the day when we received the wages for fifteen days. I had to join the gambling. That night was my night. I won almost every round from the first one. So my pocket was filled with bills very soon. However, I could not leave because of gambler's courtesy so that I stayed there playing overnight. After midnight my luck did not work any more. Oppositely I kept losing, and finally no money remained in my pocket the next morning.

I was ashamed. I could not go home with empty hands. I prayed to God, "Father, I wanted to win big money so that I can give You big offerings. But I lost all of my money. Please help me this time."

I borrowed some money and rejoined gambling. But I could not get my lost money returned.

In my village, most of the residents were laborers. They often played Hwatoo for fun.

One day the money losers gathered at my house, where we started another round of Hwatoo. Unexpectedly my church minister visited my home. I did not want to have a worship service with the minister, because I wanted to win some money through that round of Hwatoo, which would compensate my losses. So I had my wife tell a lie that I was not home. The minister shortened her visitation and left. When I heard their singing praises, it made my heart ache. I was not comfortable, feeling guilty.

'What's wrong with me? I have gladly welcomed all ministry visitors. What did I do today?' I felt so sorry for myself. My heart ached because I couldn't make my repentance immediately. Finally I was able to repent of my sin with tears. "Oh, Father! Please, please forgive me. I won't play Hwatoo any more. I will throw away my habit of gambling."

I threw away my Hwatoo cards, my desire to play Hwatoo, and my habit of lying. Since then I have never played Hwatoo, whether it was for fun or not. Instead, I disciplined myself by living according to the word of God, fasting and praying.

I prayed in a loud voice

After I stopped gambling, I willingly tried to attend as many revivals as possible. I came to have a strong faith. I believed that God would answer my prayers that I offered at the revivals. I often visited prayer houses to pray. My dream was to live according to the word of God, be blessed by God, support the poor and the sick, and evangelize to people.

One day in 1975, while I was praying in Chilbo Mountain, Suwon, I heard the voice of God for the first time. I picked that high place where I could pray in a loud voice, because it was not crowded.

"Read Luke 22:44."

The voice of God was very clear, strong and clean. Being surprised to hear His mysterious voice, I hurried to open the scripture in the Bible.

"And being in agony He was praying very fervently; and His sweat became like drops of blood, falling down upon the ground."

I wondered why God gave me this scripture. Through my prayers I came to understand the most proper way to pray.

In Israel, the daily temperature range is quite wide. Although it is summer, the temperature drops pretty low at night. It must have been almost impossible for anyone to sweat in April, around the time when Jesus was crucified. However, Jesus sweated like drops of blood falling. I could imagine how earnestly Jesus prayed. If He had prayed silently, He would not have sweated like that.

God wanted me to pray more earnestly, in anguish, like Jesus did on Gethsemane. That's why He let me hear His voice. After this happened, I prayed, following the way that God was pleased with. Then I could feel that I was filled with the Holy Spirit. I came to live by the grace and the message given from above. From this point onward, God answered my prayers more quickly.

In all things God works for the good

I had managed my life, so I could live according to God's

purpose.

My foreman, who had helped me to get the laborious job, had to move to Chunho-dong, because his illegally built house was pulled down. The government also demolished my rented house. They did not pay us any compensation, though. Worst still, my landlord refused to refund my key money on the grounds that he lost his building (my rented house) to the governmental clearing. I was sorry that my Christian landlord did not keep our rental contract because of his loss. I was wondering why God allowed him to disappoint me. Thus I had to borrow some money to rent a house at a monthly rate.

Then God provided me with a new job.

Our new rented house had a space that was suitable for a shop. We opened a shop renting books, magazines and cartoons. After a few months of operation, we moved to a shop located on the street side. However, we could not make any profit because we had to buy new books continuously and pay monthly rent. When we found we made no money, we sold our shop.

My wife and I had already put aside our greed for money. We decided to pray to God, who would bless us soon. We earnestly prayed late into the night for a whole week.

"Father, please bless us to glorify You. Please give us a shop with which we can make a lot of money."

We had no money but we had a lot of faith. A week later God answered our prayers. One of my friends told me that there was a shop for rent, under Mt. Dolsan, Gumho-dong.

We thought that this was God's blessing for us. So I went there right away and signed the contract at 800,000 Won (US $670). I still needed a lot of money to pay off the balance. When I asked a deacon to lend me some money, he said 'no' coldly. His refusal made me realize that this may not be God's blessing for us. So I met the owner of the shop to get the contract money refunded. He, after listening to my explanation, unexpectedly volunteered to lend me the balance of the money.

How wonderful God's will and love are! I should not have gone to the deacon of my church to borrow money. God had already set up everything through a non-believer.

We were experienced enough to manage the shop well. Eventually we came to desire to manage a bigger shop somewhere else.

One day a man asked me to sell my shop, which I had never put up for rent. Believing in God who guides us in everything, I sold my shop to him and surveyed the area to find a better shop to rent. The owner of the best-looking shop, located right in front of the school refused to hand it over to me, because my shop had hurt his business profit. So I rented a shop located in the back alley of Gumho-dong.

In all things God works for the good. He knew that a huge modern bookstore would move in soon across from the shop which I thought was the best. That is why God did not make the shop available for me.

My new shop had many customers. Some of them were from the shop of the owner who had refused to let me take over. Gradually customers crowded my shop till late at night.

Some of them had to read standing up. Sometimes I had to stay out of the shop to give my customers more space.

We closed the shop every Sunday, and we did not allow any student customer to drink or smoke in the shop. No one would say we set good rules. However, God's blessing was wonderful. Our customers and business profit were increasing. We could pay off almost all of our debts. And we worked hard for the church as much as possible. Our heart always desired to glorify God through financial blessing.

My wife and I worked hard during the daytime and prayed earnestly at night. We could dream that everything would surely come true.

My servant I had chosen before time began!

When I was praying in May, I heard the voice of God clearly.

"My servant whom I had chosen before time began! I have refined you for three years. Now, prepare yourself for the word over the next three years. You have loved Me more than your parents, brothers, sisters, wife and children. Leave the current business now and go your way. Let your wife manage the shop."

His voice was clear and loud yet gentle and warm. He continued speaking to.

"My thoughts are not the same as man's. Your wife will earn more money than you and your wife earned together. Your family will lend to many people but will borrow from none. A good measure, pressed down, shaken together and

running over, will be poured into your lap.

Do as I told you. Then your rice container will never be empty and your cash box will always be full.

After you arm yourself with the word for three years, you will go across rivers and oceans and do miracles and wonders."

I was shocked to know that God called me as His servant; I had never planned to be. I clearly understood that it was God's calling on me to be His servant. But my mind was not ready for it.

'I have prayed so many times to be an elder so as to glorify God... not as a servant of God. How can I be His servant? I am quite old and my memory is poor. How can I study theology at the school?'

I was wondering why God told me that. I wanted to obey as God said, but I did not know how to obey. I felt overwhelmingly lost.

If you can?

My heart ached with the conflict. I desired to obey God, but I could not. I was so sorry that I could not obey God. Two bells were echoing in my mind, fighting with each other. 'Obedience is better than sacrifice.' 'How dare I become a servant of God?'

I could not stay working at my shop. I packed my stuff and went to a prayer mountain to find peace in my heart.

"Father, should I become a pastor? If it is surely Your will, please let me hear Your voice once again. Then I will obey You with confidence."

I fasted and prayed earnestly, but I could not hear His voice. I felt exhausted as I was coming down from the mountain. I was like a dead man.

I visited some more prayer mountains, but still God did not give me any clear answer. My heart ached more and more as time passed. One month, two months, three months... I was really eager to hear God's answer.

My wandering ended

"Oh, Father! I will obey what You told me, if it is Your will. I will become one of Your servants, if I must. I can do it, if You tell it to me again."

It was Saturday night when I was completing my seven days of overnight praying. I was in such a dilemma that I did not think I would be able to make the representative prayer at the worship service the next day, unless I would hear God's voice again. I was crying out to God with all my heart. Right then, God did tell me. The Holy Spirit gave me a clear realization. "Do the representative prayer." *"What do you mean by 'If you can?' Everything is possible for those who believe. To obey is better than sacrifice. I see man's heart and not his appearance."*

How joyful it was! I felt that I owned everything in the world. It was like flying in the air, feeling weightless. It was beyond description for me to say how delighted I was.

"God delivered you from misery and pain. He thoroughly

healed you and guided you to love the Lord only. He gave you faith to believe, the ability to pray, and strength to live by the word. He helped you to have a sweet home, blessed you financially, and supplied you all the things you needed.

God called you to be His servant, because He knew you could do it. God considered you righteous enough to be His servant, because you love God more than anything or anyone. God wants you to live according to the word only and give glory to Him. God is so pleased with your heart that He has called you to be His servant."

My joy lasted up to the Sabbath Day. I was filled with the I-can-do-it spirit. I decided to devote myself to being a servant of God.

My three months of wandering ended. It was early September in 1978. My wife quit her sales job and managed our bookshop to follow God's instructions. Her income was amazingly increased in a few weeks to over 600,000 Won (US $500) a month.

Her bookshop gained a good reputation so that some shop managers came to see what kind of special sales skills my wife had. None of their curiosity was answered, because my wife operated her shop with some negative looking policies:

1. She screens customers - no disrespectful students admitted.

2. She closes the shop every Sunday.

They could not understand why my wife had so many customers. Neither could they understand God, who created everything from nothing. He blessed my wife, who kept every

Sabbath, living in truth, spreading the gospel, and praising God, while she managed the shop.

God blessed my wife to make more money than we made together before. He blessed us abundantly because He was pleased with our obedience.

You scored 100% on the Bible

I rented a separate room for myself while I prepared for the theology school exam. Rev. Younghoon Yi, from Sungdong Church where I had served as a deacon, advised me to go to Sungkyul (Holiness) Theology School. I began to study for the entrance exam. I wanted to pass the exam and score a 100 % on the Bible test, because I would become a servant of God. To aid my desire I repeatedly fasted for ten days and then twenty-one days.

"Dear Father, please accept my fasting and give me the ability to memorize everything I have studied. Please help me understand clearly what I read in the Bible and memorize everything that I read. In the name of the Lord, who revived the dead, I pray."

From the first day, I knelt and began to read the Bible very carefully. While reading the Bible that was written through the inspiration of the Holy Spirit, I also felt inspired.

Finally test day came. I had only studied the Bible. I did not try to answer the questions about any other subject. My answer sheets were blank except for the Bible, which I answered 100%.

The next day we were to have an interview. The college president asked me, "Why did you submit your answer sheets blank except for the one on the Bible? Wait a minute, you've got 100 % on the Bible!"

The school was reluctant to deal with my admission, but God allowed me to enter.

After I entered the theology school, I often prayed overnight and fasted. My fasting days numbered more than my regular days, and I seldom celebrated my birthday or holidays.

This occurred during my freshman year.

I was in the middle of the overnight prayer schedule that I made a promise to God to keep. I saw an announcement for the semester final exam. I felt like I was in trouble, because although I was great at the Bible, I couldn't remember anything in English or Greek. Besides, I promised God I would pray overnight for more nights. So I begged God for His help. I had no choice but to pray. "Father, I promised to pray overnight before I knew the exam schedule. Please help me do both of them well. I believe that You help me to pray and take the exam well."

When I prayed for an hour, God supplied me the test questions. I studied those questions for an hour and finished the daily overnight prayer schedule.

The next day was the exam. When I opened the test paper, I was surprised. All of the questions were the same as those God had showed me. How amazing His help and guidance are! I gave all thanks and glory to God.

I received a divine revelation of the end

I was completing 21 days of overnight prayer in the last week of June 1979. It was 4 o'clock in the morning. Thanking God, I was about to close my prayer when God gave me a divine revelation concerning the end. *"My dear servant, stay awake and be prudent. The end is near."*

I had prayed for my exact understanding of the scriptures:

"But the day of the Lord will come like a thief" (2 Peter 3:10).

"But you, brethren, are not in darkness, that the day would overtake you like a thief" (1 Thessalonians 5:4).

When I prayed about the scripture Amos 3:7, *"Surely the LORD God does nothing Unless He reveals His secret counsel To His servants the prophets."* God told me that through the Bible He lets the believers know about the Second Coming of the Lord. He told me that the day is near and I must keep watch and get ready for it (Matthew 24:42-44). He also talked to me about the signs of the end.

Even though only God knows when the end is, we can recognize through prophecy given in the Bible that the day is near. Therefore, we must always stay awake. If not, the day will sneak upon us like a thief. Then we may lose the opportunity to be saved.

Noah's case is a good example. People were indulging in eating, drinking and getting married until Noah entered the ark to escape the waters of the flood, and they all perished. Since they were not awake, the day of destruction came upon them like a thief.

Likewise, the faithful believers will prepare themselves for the day to come soon. However, the day will come like a thief upon non-believers or the chaff-like believers who are associated with the world, because they do not realize that the day is near.

They cannot receive salvation.

One day, one of my classmates talked to me about his dream. "I had a strange dream. In my dream you told me, 'We don't know when the Lord will come again. So stay awake, because the day is near.'"

Through his dream, God confirmed the revelation He had given me before.

Afterwards I double-checked scriptures with the revelation God gave me. Every statement God had spoken to me was confirmed with the scriptures. I was overjoyed.

In August of my freshman year, I participated in the summer camp at Canaan Farming School, where my favorite pastor was with us. I had respected pastors as I serve Jesus. However, they disappointed me.

One day we were discussing the adultery based on Matthew 5:27-28, *"You have heard that it was said, 'You shall not commit adultery'; but I say to you that everyone who looks at a woman with lust for her has already committed adultery with her in his heart."* Eventually their heated discussion led to a sophisticated conclusion—If you have lustful thinking in your mind only, you are not committing the sin of adultery. I was shocked to hear them, because I succeeded in getting rid of adultery in my mind through three years of prayer.

I deeply thanked God for my successful fight of my past days.

"Father, thank You so much! If I had heard that adultery in our minds was not conquerable, I would have kept it until the day I die. But You have guided me to live according to the word, fighting against the sin of adultery for many years."

My decision to rely on and follow the word of God only was becoming intense and concrete.

Some of the seminary students opened churches before they graduated. I also wanted to. To make my dream come true I gave twenty-one days of fasting to God during summer vacation. I did not feel comfortable with opening a church, because I still had several questions relating to biblical verses I had not fully understood yet. Neither professors nor good commentary bibles could answer my questions. No one gave me a satisfactory answer.

Since I, as a new Christian, attended the revival in November 1974, I have prayed whenever I have had free time.

"Dear Father, I want You to explain the Bible to me Yourself. I know You can help me through angels. Please work on me in Your way so that I may understand all of Your 66 books of the Bible."

My 40 days of fasting

During the winter vacation in 1981, God worked on me to do 40 days of fasting with prayer. I was sure that I did not set this plan of fasting, but God did. As I was praying for the preparation of my fasting, God said to me, "My dear servant! Do not read any other books except for the Bible and hymnbook."

I was about to pack some books that would help me get armed with the word. I put the other books aside and went to the Osanri Prayer Mountain to fast and pray. As I began the fast, I thought God would help me so that I could endure and complete it without any problem. I prayed that I might become a servant to please God as a powerful pastor, become armed with the word, and be able to open a church.

God did not help me until I reached the fortieth day. I could not sleep well, and I often had cramps in my arms and legs. When it turned thirty days, I felt dizzy much of the time. Sometimes blood came up when I vomited. I could not drink water because of the severe pain in my throat.

When I turned over to the fortieth day, my pain seemed to be the worst. Ten minutes seemed like an hour to me. Although I was very cold, dizzy, aching, weak and exhausted, God helped me to keep my daily schedule, two hours of praying in a loud voice.

Finally at 11 o'clock PM on Day 40, all my pains disappeared. It was miraculous. God let me have victory as I fought against the temptation of Satan, who had tried to stop me from the seventh day.

All of my family sang and danced together. We had a worship service to give thanks and glory to God. He had watched me with His fiery eyes up to the last day of my fasting and gave me the strength to complete the 40 days. How wonderful He is! Tears streamed down my face as I thanked God.

"All the glory be to You, God!"

After this period of fasting, God opened the way for me to completely understand all sixty-six books of the Bible.

Starting a church

"Behold, I stand at the door and knock; if anyone hears My voice and opens the door, I will come in to him and will dine with him, and he with Me" (Revelation 3:20).

God, who had me experience miracles, called and came into me, and began to change me into a man of God.

In April 1974, God blessed me with the knowledge that He is alive. Since then, I have attended church and received His grace and love. At the beginning I did not know how to pray because no one taught me.

In November 1974, I attended a revival, where I became filled with the Holy Spirit as I listened to the sermon and the testimony, praising and praying to God. Through my repentance I realized that I was a sinner. I also realized that the love of God and the grace of the Lord who was crucified, are immeasurable. Every message tasted like honey to me, and I was blessed to be able to pray faithfully and to have God answer all my prayers.

After I attended the revival and realized that I was a sinner, I tried to pray as much as I could. God guided me to live according to His word. He comforted and disciplined me. He gave me understanding so that I changed and lived my life as His child.

God made me throw away my sinful cravings, the lust of my eyes, and the pride of my worldly life. He changed me into a person who loves God, loves my neighbors like myself, and serves God with all my heart. Just as my soul prospered, all went well with me, and I was in great health. I became a good Christian, giving the glory to God, making testimonies, and spreading the gospel.

From the day my wife left me on 10 July, 1974, God had disciplined me for three years to get rid of my sinful nature. As a result, I became a man of God, rejoicing always, giving thanks to God in everything, and praying earnestly.

Before 9 July, 1977, my family bought only the smallest bag of rice so that we could pay off all our debts without failing to give regular offerings to God.

Although we would have no food for the next day, we served all the food that we had to servants of God and visitors who came to see my family. Then, God never failed to work for my family. He sent someone with food the very next day, so no one in my family had to skip any meals.

As of 9 July, 1977 when my wife and I opened the shop for the third time, God blessed my family so abundantly that we could glorify Him by financially supporting people in need and giving voluntary services to the church.

As a servant of God

In May 1978, God called me as His servant and told me to prepare for the word. Since then I have lived my life, fasting, praying overnight, and keeping the commandments as the Bible says in order to become armed with His word.

God armed me with powerful prayer, revelation and miraculous healing, so that I was getting to be His servant who would guide people toward salvation.

While I was a seminary student, God helped me to arm myself with the word and prayer during vacations. He also worked on me while I was at home to counsel many types of visitors about various topics.

God gave me spiritual training through miraculous power of the Holy Spirit that appeared through me. I gained valuable experience while I was a deacon. I visited several churches and prayed for those who were in trouble or sick.

From May 1981, I focused my prayer, concentrating mainly on opening a church. And I learned about the ministerial jobs relating to elementary, middle and high school students, young adults, college students and married adults. I also learned about relevant church affairs, how to operate a church and choir, and how to organize the faculty. For more useful practical experience I went to another church I liked, volunteered to help them, and preached several times.

The last week of February 1982 marked the completion of three years that God told me to study and become armed with the word. During this week, which was the last week before I started my senior year of school, God led me to hold a revival for the first time in my life, at Ilman Church in Masan City. It was a great opportunity for me to hold a revival, which made my desire for starting a church even stronger. My prayers for starting a church became stronger and deeper.

In May 1982, one by one, God began to answer my prayers for starting a church. One day a new church member, whom my wife guided to our church two weeks ago, visited me without notice.

"Pastor, someone called me last night three times and woke me up. The light was so bright and beautiful that I couldn't keep my eyes open to see God who appeared. He said to me, 'I chose you and I will make you my witness to testify to the world about me.' I don't understand what this means."

She did not know anything of the scriptures, Genesis or Matthew. If she knew anything, it was the names of God and Jesus. Her stomach disease was healed after I prayed for her just once.

She came to me a few days later.

"Pastor, I saw another strange scene in my dream. You waved your right hand to call me to you. You told me to hold your hand and took me to a warehouse with red roof. There were a lot of sacks filled with gold in the warehouse. I asked you, 'What is in the gold?' You answered me, 'Salt is in it.' You handed me two bars of gold and said, 'Keep them until you will use them significantly.' You took me back to the place where you waved to call me. You looked around all four directions and said to me, 'We are to go together in God from now until our Lord comes, passing fields, going over mountains and crossing over rivers to spread the gospel of God.'"

I believed that God had a special plan for her. So I often prayed for her and guided her with the word of truth.

In April 1982, my wife was cultivating her qualifications for the wife of a Pastor. As a cell leader, she increased her cell members from four4 to twenty-eight within five months. Her prayer was getting more powerful and she took good care of her cell members with love. She led meetings, sharing the bread of love, closely associated with others, and spread the gospel to many.

God had me hold four prayer meeting times and sent me the necessary workers for the church I was going to start. He, who created everything from nothing, did not want me to start the church in my own human will. Although I had some Christian family members - my eldest sister (deaconess), my second sister (minister), a sister-in-law (my wife's brother's wife) and my wife's sister, God did not want me to rely on my family or relatives, but sent to me, right on time, the workers He had prepared.

God also took care of all our financial needs. Our bookshop did not make any profit for us any more. We started to lose money, including the key money deposit, because we could not pay the monthly rent. With faith I asked God for help. How wonderful! God had already prepared Deaconess Aeja Ahn with the money needed.

Another blessing was that God gave me a prophetess. It was God's answer to my seven years of prayer. I had prayed that God would reveal every verse of all 66 books of the Scripture to me.

Additionally, God showed miraculous signs through me.

As I mentioned above, God furnished me with all I needed and told me to start the church on a sizzling hot day. He did not miss telling me that I would have to take a test upon starting the church.

I was about to receive the answer to seven years of prayer for starting a church. Of course Satan began to attack me, tearing at me like a lion trying to rip me to pieces.

The test upon starting the church

It was in the middle of June, my senior year at the college where I studied theology.

The pastor, who was in charge of my class, asked one of my classmates if there was anything theologically wrong with any one of the seniors. He answered the pastor that a few seniors including me seemed to have problems. This inaccurate personal survey came to produce rumors relating to a prophetic statement while attending a prayer meeting at Mt. Samgak.

The rumors were: A woman laid her hands on a servant of God. The servant of God asked the woman to lay her hands on him. The servant of God called himself 'The Christ.'

These rumors caused some tests for me before starting a church.

A woman had never laid hands on any servant of God at that meeting. No servant of God asked the woman to lay her hands on him. And I had never said, 'I am the Christ.' But the rumors produced new rumors. The final rumor was that I was heretical. My school called a meeting to discuss my expulsion. I did not know what was going on until Rev. K, who trusted me, informed me.

Some of my church members were spreading a similar rumor - Avoid Minister Jaerock Lee. He is a heretic.

I was okay in my heart, because I was ready to endure any type of test for starting a church. However, I was trembling to hear that my school was trying to expel me.

The next day was the final exam, followed by summer vacation. I did not go to school, and instead, I went to the church with some witnesses to tell them the true story. However, they did not try to listen to my explanation.

At the semester-end ceremony, those students, who tried to defend me, received a warning from the administration.

The administration said about me, 'He is demon-possessed' 'His power comes from the devil' and 'He is a heretic.' I just prayed with faith because I remembered the prophecy given to me: *"Do not worry. Give thanks for everything and pray. The troops of Satan will break down. Do not hate but love them always."*

The time came, and God gave me a great blessing in reward

for my endurance. He made everything work together for the good so that I had no problem with starting a church.

As it was prophesied, I fasted for three days and then went out to find the place where I would start the church. The building I found had no other church nearby and was standing with a good view around. I waited for an hour for the building owner who would come to sign the contract. I prayed to God.

"Father, I've waited for the building owner for an hour. If she doesn't show up within five minutes, I'll leave and consider this not what you want me to do."

What a surprise! The landlord showed up in a minute! It looked miraculous to me.

She said, "I came here to tell you that I don't want to rent it to you. But when I saw your face, I changed my mind. I don't know why."

Although Satan tried to interfere with the landlord and the contract, I won. This experience taught me again that the will of God never fails.

As God told me before, *"You will start the church on a day when it is sizzling hot,"* I gave the first worship service in Shindaebang-dong, Dongjak-gu on 25 July, 1982. The attendants were our thirteen members (nine adults + four children).

My deep impression of the first service

I had been called 'heretic' and almost expelled from the college. So I was deeply impressed by the starting service. I kept shouting 'Hallelujah!' and crying with gratitude.

After we started the church, our members came to earnestly pray together for urgent topics. Our five core members prayed in a loud voice for five or six hours every day. God said in Jeremiah 33:3, *"Call to Me and I will answer you, and I will tell you great and mighty things, which you do not know."*

As God said, He sent us new people, provided us with the pulpit, piano, telephone and other things we all needed.

Since we started the church, we have not missed giving the Friday overnight service with praising and praying. As we have rejoiced with thanks and prayer according to His will, God has shown thousands of miracles, solved our physical and spiritual problems, blessed us with the opportunity to meet Him, and sent many people and workers.

Many members were healed of their stomach cancers, lymph infections, heart diseases and malignant stomach diseases, and have been working devotedly for the church.

Our members have lived by the word of God and given the glory to Him, keeping the Sabbath holy. God has been pleased with us so that He has sent us new members every week so far with the exception of only one week.

All these occurrences have shown the power of God, who created everything from nothing, and has guided and worked in us.

The vessel

"Now in a large house there are not only gold and silver vessels, but also vessels of wood and of earthenware, and some to honor and some to dishonor. Therefore, if anyone cleanses himself from these things he will be a vessel for honor, sanctified, useful to the Master, prepared for every good work" (2 Timothy 2:20-21).

Becoming a great vessel

It had taken three full years for my dream to come true.

Since my elder sister promised me to donate some land for a church building, I tried many ways to start a church. I submitted the paper work for constructing a building, but I could not get approval. I tried to borrow the money needed to rent a room in a building, but I could not borrow any money either.

Member-wise, I had no problem with starting a church. More than ten people, including my elder sisters and their children were tentatively ready to attend. I did not think there was any problem with starting a church if I got help from my family members and relatives. However, that was not God's will.

God said in Proverbs 16:9, *"The mind of man plans his way, but the LORD directs his steps."* I planned my course by myself, but did not let God determine my steps. Although I verbally said that I put everything in God's hands, my thoughts led my course before God did. But it was not long until I gave everything back to God, following as God led and worked.

Then God brought us a miraculous result with His power.

I prayed for the name of the church for a long time. God did not answer me until I became the vessel who was eligible enough to be blessed. Finally He told me to name the church 'Manmin (all creation).'

"Go into all the world and preach the gospel to all creation" (Mark 16:15).

When God called me as His servant, He told me that I would show miraculous signs and wonders, traveling over mountains, rivers and oceans. Now He is giving me another task; *"Start a church in the way God created everything from nothing, and be a great vessel that is able to preach the gospel to all creation."*

As God wanted, our church started only with the people and funds that God had prepared. I did not get any help from my brothers, sisters or relatives. I realized again in my heart that God is almighty. I deeply thanked Him for His miraculous work.

The enemy Satan and the devil tried to obstruct us from starting a church, but God gave us the final victory.

To accomplish His kingdom God prepared various vessels, not only of gold and silver, but also of wood and clay; some for noble purposes and some for ignoble. If a man cleanses himself, he will be an instrument for noble purposes, made holy, useful to the Master and prepared to do any good work.

I was wondering what kind of vessel I was and how I could be a useful vessel to God.

Clean vessel

Until the day when God had me start the church, God helped me become a clean vessel. God helped me not to commit any sins but be sanctified. I kept all of the Ten Commandments so that I bore the nine fruit of the Holy Spirit.

On the other hand, God gave me time to refine myself through sufferings. The prophetess who God had sent brought an unexpectedly hard trial to me. I had many ministerial acquaintances that experienced the miraculous works of God and prayed together with me. One of them made a false testimony. This incident caused my theology school administrators to regard me as a heretic. Although I was almost expelled from the school, I just followed what God taught in the Bible.

"Be anxious for nothing, but in everything by prayer and supplication with thanksgiving let your requests be made known to God. And the peace of God, which surpasses all comprehension, will guard your hearts and your minds in Christ Jesus" (Philippians 4:6-7).

In this world there are several kinds of people. Some people try to sell out their countries, but some are so loyal as to give their lives. Everybody has his own vessel. I believed in God who would help me. That is why I kept praying to the end. Eventually good won over evil. Truth overcame devils.

God watched me pass the last trial, overcome sins, and live a pure life. He, at last, determined I was eligible to start a church.

Some of my junior ministers talked about that time. "We trembled in our shoes, but you did not care how the situation went. You just kept praying boldly. You never hated any of them. Your faith was more than great."

My wife also talked about that time. "You know, I was almost crazy for the last few months before we started the church. I didn't know what to do in our struggle against that fiery trial. However, you were different from us, Reverend."

God had Satan admit that I was a clean vessel so I was able to start a church. And then God showed us that He is almighty. After we overcame the trials, God gave us such abundant blessings that we could not even count them.

God who answers our prayers like fire

After we started the church, God made me clearly understand His providence while I was praying like a burning fire. Since then, my church members and I started to pray for the world mission.

As Jesus called twelve disciples to accomplish the will of God, God sent good workers to our church in time to accomplish God's will and providence.

One day God showed us the image of the Grand Sanctuary which we would build. God showed seventeen members and me the features of the Grand Sanctuary in great detail. We saw the roof, ninethy-six marble pillars and the inside of the sanctuary. The stage was set in the center of the interior, and the pulpit was turning slowly. God showed us my images preaching to countless people who are receiving grace and conducting miracles. By showing these scenes God encouraged us to pray with faith for the world mission.

God blessed me to become a great vessel in which many ministers and members may come and rest. When I was called as a servant of God, I was lost, not knowing what to do, so I wandered for three months. But God molded me to become a pastor who dreams of a world mission, praying with faith and deeds. How wonderfully God had changed me!

Again, God blessed me to become a powerful leader so that numerous people came and rested in me.

Although I was a new Christian, if I prayed for sick people, miraculously they were healed.

I had an opportunity to listen to a testimony.

"My son scalded himself with very hot boiling water. His scald was so severe that no medical treatment could cure him for a long time.

One day I remembered King Asa as described in chapter 16, 2 Chronicles. He died because in his illness he did not seek help from the LORD, but only from the physicians. I decided to seek help from God and prayed and fasted. God healed my son completely! Hallelujah!"

I had my own experience with being healed. I believed the parent's testimony. So I prayed to God for whatever I needed. I was sure that praying brings a solution. When my daughters got sick, I prayed for them, and they were healed. Their fever disappeared right away. These healing experiences happily encouraged me. For several days I fasted and prayed about my healing power. Since then, every time I prayed for the sick, they got healed. It was really amazing.

After I was called as a servant of God, my prayer topics were opening a church, becoming armed with the word of God, receiving power and gifts, being armed with prayers and being sanctified. God answered my prayers before I opened the church. He gave me not only the nine spiritual gifts but also the gifts of love, reading minds and vision. God gave me the power to heal all kinds of diseases, including incurable illnesses, barrenness and demon-possession. God showed His healing power through me and blessed me to know the laws of the spiritual realm.

Right after starting the church, God sent me various kinds of sick people - paralytic, cancer, arthritis, heart disease, lymphatic inflammation, tuberculosis, stomach diseases and the blind. God thoroughly healed them.

Any kind of disease God can heal! Because He is almighty!

God also sent me those people who were poor in spirit, who misunderstood the word, who were in suffering because of their disobedience, who were wandering here and there for lack of spiritual strength. God endowed me with healing power so that I could take care of them completely.

God who fills the vessels as they are

God blessed me as much as I cultivated my vessel according

to His will. My congregation upon starting was nine, but it increased to more than 100 on October 10th, when we had the official opening service. And it has increased rapidly year by year to become one of the biggest churches in the world.

Why has God blessed me and increased my church members so dramatically? I believe that God has made me a great vessel to glorify Him because I have lived a holy life and always obeyed His will.

I had a big dream to preach the gospel to many people. I wanted to guide many people to salvation in order to please God, who would complement me. I prayed for this dream for a long time.

Realizing that anyone who wishes to be a clean and great vessel must have suitable wisdom, I did my best to be so.

"Who among you is wise and understanding? Let him show by his good behavior his deeds in the gentleness of wisdom" (James 3:13).

"But the wisdom from above is first pure, then peaceable, gentle, reasonable, full of mercy and good fruits, unwavering, without hypocrisy. And the seed whose fruit is righteousness is sown in peace by those who make peace" (James 3:17-18).

I showed my good deeds according to the wisdom God gave me.

I often provided financial aid to other developing churches, gave offerings for the theology school construction, and supported servants of God with housing and tuition aid programs so that they could devote themselves only to the church.

We offered lunch to the entire congregation every Sunday, so they had gracious fellowship and kept the Sabbath without doing anything else all day. Our financial condition did not allow for that, but I never worried about anything. I just obeyed Him as He said, *"Give and you will be filled again. Those who sow little will reap little, but those who sow much will reap much."*

I concentrated my whole attention upon praying, communicating with God and receiving revelation from God in order to lead a great number of people to salvation and to glorify God.

God gave me full comprehension of the difficult passages in all sixty-six books of the Bible. I decided to devote myself to spreading the good news to every end of the world, and put my heart and soul into cultivating members, turning the chaff into the grain, and non-believers into believers, until the day our Lord comes again.

5

GOD HAS ACCOMPANIED ME

The blessed

"How blessed is the man who does not walk in the counsel of the wicked, nor stand in the path of sinners, nor sit in the seat of scoffers! But his delight is in the law of the LORD, and in His law he meditates day and night. He will be like a tree firmly planted by streams of water, which yields its fruit in its season and its leaf does not wither; and in whatever he does, he prospers" *(Psalm 1:1-3).*

The truly blessed

It is natural that everyone living in this world wants to be blessed. Many Korean parents name their newborn children 'Boknam' (Blessed Boy) or 'Boksoon' (Blessed Girl).

While I was ill, I even visited a famous name composer to select a better name. I had to stay there in a long line until it

147

was my turn to see the famous man, Bongsoo Kim. He examined my face and my wife's face with our names and said to us, "Jaerock is fated to die young, and Boknim will live a hard life like a housemaid. I've never seen such bad names before."

He gave us new names, 'Sung-ook' for me, and 'Jeeyon' for my wife. What happened afterwards? My diseases did not leave me and my wife still had to live a hard life.

When my wife was born, she was named 'Boknim' which means 'She is blessed.' Later, as the name composer advised, she changed her name to 'Jeeyon', because she heard that her original name was interpreted 'to become a housemaid.' But nothing like blessing came to her.

How earnestly had we exerted ourselves to get blessings? Even our constant devotion looked miserable. 'How can I get healthy?' 'How can I earn big money and get out of poverty?' 'How can we have our poor daughters well taken care of?' We always had thoughts of blessings.

People say that to be blessed means to live a long, healthy, rich and peaceful life with many children. They say richness is the key blessing. So they think they will live a good life if they are rich and healthy. But what if they die? Nothing is valuable for them. Their luck is needed just for their lifetime, for about 70 to 80 years. Eventually their luck disappears. It cannot be a true blessing.

What is a true blessing? What kind of blessing lasts forever although we die? The Bible, in which the history of mankind, their lives, deaths, fortunes and misfortunes are written, has described the true blessing.

"And I will make you a great nation, and I will bless you, and make your name great; and so you shall be a blessing" (Genesis 12:2).

Here, the blessed man is Abraham. He believed in God the Creator who rules everything. He obeyed as God commanded, and his ways were blameless.

Abraham lived to the ripe old age of 175. He had no child, but God blessed him later to have many children, who grew up in obedience. He also had many servants, flocks and goods. He was blessed in all things. And Abraham, more than all the above, received eternal life as the father of faith after he died.

The greatest blessing stated in the Bible is the spiritual one that is given to those who believe in and obey God, live according to the word, and go to heaven where there is no tear, sorrow or pain. The second best blessing is the one necessary to the worldly life, such as getting along well with everything, good health, long life, children, honor and wealth.

To be truly blessed means to receive both of these blessings.

There are a lot of people who seemed to be blessed. Around us we can see that the worldly blessings do not last long. Some people, who used to have many cars and houses, spent their money like water, and suddenly become penniless or starved. Some of them die young, leaving a great fortune. Some of them accidentally lose their wives and children. We cannot say they are blessed.

Just the opposite, heavenly blessing is not temporary but permanent. The more days pass, the more blessings come. This is the true blessing. I am a witness to that.

The blessings I have received

God blessed me as much as my vessel changed. Here I'd like to describe how much and how wonderfully God blessed me.

I lived for a long time, not knowing that God exists and there is eternal life after death. I thought death was the end of life. So I had no hope that there was anything special about life.

One day I came to experience that God is alive. Once I met God, I believed that He and His kingdom exist. Then I repented of my ignorance and foolishness. I admitted that I was a sinner and decided to live according to the word of God. I was so happy to realize that I received the most significant blessing of salvation. Since then, my lips always sang praises, prayed and thanked God for everything.

Secondly, after I met God, my ruggedly torn sick body was thoroughly healed. God gave me a healthy body and a sweet home with bright children. Furthermore, He called me as His servant, who would preach the gospel, serve the church, the body of Jesus Christ, guide people to salvation, and work together with Him as a man of God.

Thirdly, I was blessed to be with God always. God has never left me alone because I have pleased Him. How wonderful His blessing is! To accompany the president of your country must be very honorable. How honorable will it be to get accompanied by the almighty God? It is tremendously honorable and worthwhile.

Parents accompany their children, feed them when they are hungry, dress them, accommodate them where they sleep, supply them the things they need, and protect them from danger.

Likewise, God has accompanied me, providing me with things I needed and endowing me with the authority and the power so that I could work for His kingdom and righteousness.

The demon-possessed trembled upon looking at me. God made all of my words come true, so my congregation trusted and obeyed me. Whenever I prayed for my church members, God showed us His miraculous power.

The fourth blessing God gave me was that I received from God whatever I asked for.

Whatever I asked for

It had been about six months since we started the church. At that time, the sanctuary was on the second floor, and my home and office were in the basement.

It was one day prior to the big holiday 'Sullal' (Lunar New Year), at about 6 o'clock in the morning when we were finishing the Friday Overnight Service. There a serious bustle was taking place. It was carbon monoxide poisoning. My three young daughters and a young adult member who was too tired to attend the Friday overnight service were sleeping in my home in the basement. When they were found, they looked dead. They had fallen unconscious and their bodies were cold and solid. My church members were moving here and there, not knowing what to do. I told them to bring those gas-poisoned people into the church. I went up to the altar and prayed.

"Father, I thank You. Whether You take my three daughters now or not, I thank You. If I have done anything wrong, please let me know and forgive me. Father, here I have a young man. He is a member of my congregation. Please save this young man so that we may not disgrace your name."

I came down from the altar, laid my hands on the young man and prayed. "In the name of Jesus Christ of Nazareth I command! You, charcoal gas, be gone! Come out of him! I command you! Come out of his body! Father, please bring him back to life and let us glorify Your name."

I then prayed over my three daughters one by one. While I was praying for my daughters, the young man sat up and wondered what had happened. My three daughters also sat up in a row. Hallelujah!

Seeing this miracle, my church members' faith grew stronger than before and gave all glory to God who makes impossible things possible to those who believe in Him. Since then, there have been many people who were gas-poisoned but came back to life through my prayers.

Here is another miracle.

Our high school students and young adult members were about to depart for the summer camp that was planned for the first time since we opened our church. It was early morning. It had been raining heavily overnight. The rain became heavier with thunder and lightning. The students and young adult members, who brought their baggage to the church the previous night, looked so disappointed.

I asked God. "Father, we're leaving for the summer camp today. I know You control the weather. Would You please stop this thunder, lightning and rain so that my students and young adult members may have a great summer camp this time?"

We prayed loudly all together and asked God with faith. What happened next? God answered our prayers and stopped the heavy rain.

Our camp destination was Daeboo-do Island near Inchon. There was only one ferryboat service a day available. We were supposed to leave the church by 5 o'clock in the morning. However, the rain was still pouring until 4:55. I believed that God would do something for us. So I asked them.

"My dear young members, do you believe that if we pray loudly for three minutes, God will stop the thunder, lightning and heavy rain?"

All of them said, 'Amen!'

After three minutes of prayer I told them to go. And all of us came downstairs. The very moment when we took the first step on the ground, the rain stopped. It was unbelievable! Just one second ago, it was thundering, lightning and raining heavily. Who can believe this actually happened?

Our almighty God changed the weather for us. What other things would He not be willing to do for us? He had given us whatever we asked.

> *"If you abide in Me, and My words abide in you, ask whatever you wish, and it will be done for you" (John 15:7).*

The blessings are given not only to me but also to those who believe in God, living a holy life according to the word.

We can ask this question of ourselves. Have those people who call, 'Lord, Lord!' received the blessings? Have all those who call themselves Christian received the blessings?

I hope that all of you may live by the word of God so that all things go well as your souls go well. I also hope that you may be healthy and live your lives going together with God, who may answer every prayer of yours.

The voice of the Lord

> *"All things have been handed over to Me by My Father, and no one knows who the Son is except the Father, and who the Father is except the Son, and anyone to whom the Son wills to reveal Him. Turning to the disciples, He said privately, 'Blessed are the eyes which see the things you see, for I say to you, that many prophets and*

kings wished to see the things which you see, and did not see them, and to hear the things which you hear, and did not hear them'" (Luke 10:22-24).

Recently a lot of teachers and parents say that it is so hard to handle teenagers. Most of those teenagers who make trouble come from loveless homes where there is no communication between parents and their children. For lack of communication, those children cannot feel parental love so that they cannot follow their parents' guidance. Eventually they are apt to go toward the pitfalls of life.

If we live our lives being accompanied by God, we can have deep love and communication with Him, hear His voice, know clearly and obey His will so that we may glorify God by accomplishing many duties for which God will reward us.

As the children of God, if we cannot communicate with Him, how desperate and depressed will we be? Life would be like living with a deaf and mute father.

God lets us hear His voice during His communication with us. The voice of God can be heard in many ways. Based on my experiences, let me explain about the different ways you can hear God.

The voice of the Holy Spirit

Before you accept Jesus as your Savior, you live by your own principles. If you have a good conscience, you will not do evil things. However, if you become affected by the bad things you see or you think of, you will live a vicious life because your conscience will become more evil.

Let's say there is something right next to you that you like very much. It does not belong to you, but you can steal it.

Here, your good conscience will say, "To take something without permission is stealing. You must not do it." So you would not steal it because you heard the voice of good conscience. Oppositely, the evil conscience will say, "Come on. No one knows. Everybody steals in this situation. Take it. It will be no problem." If you listen to the voice of the evil one, you would steal. Everybody differs in what voice he or she hears.

If you are accustomed to listening to the good conscience, you will believe in Jesus, attend church, and hear the word of God. The word of God never changes in any situation because it is the truth.

If you open your heart and accept Jesus Christ as your Savior, you will receive the Holy Spirit as a gift. And the truth, which came to you through thought, will revive your spirit. This spiritual phenomenon comes after you receive the Holy Spirit.

The Holy Spirit teaches you who the Lord is, what the truth is, and what sin is. So if you, according to the word, throw away the sinful nature, your spirit becomes able to hear the voice of the Holy Spirit. And then when you throw away all of your sins and become holy, you will hear the voice of the Holy Spirit very clearly.

There are three ways the Holy Spirit speaks to you.

The first one is the voice that makes you realize the truth. Although you have decided not to hate anyone, if you see someone you do not like, hatred arises in your heart. At this moment, the Holy Spirit gives you the realization through the word, *"If someone says, 'I love God,' and hates his brother, he is a liar; for the one who does not love his brother whom he has seen, cannot love God whom he has not seen"* (1 John 4:20).

If you hear this type of voice and comfort your heart so that you try to love and pray for the person you do not like, your hatred will unknowingly change to love.

The second one is the voice that makes you feel uncomfortable in order to let you know the will of God. When you happened to occasionally tell a lie to one of your friends, the Holy Spirit makes you feel uncomfortable so that you realize you are committing a sin. Likewise, the Holy Spirit gives you uneasiness when you violate the word.

There is a similar voice that can make you feel uncomfortable although you do not violate the word of God.

Sometimes God, who is almighty, will forcefully have you do something. Then you would feel a sudden urge to pray, go home or do something unusual. That is because God protects you from danger and leads you to go along well with all things. If you feel uneasy while you are waiting for the bus, it is because the Holy Spirit is speaking to you not to take the bus.

This one happened on a Sunday while I was a deacon.

I intended to go to the second service because of the laymen meeting. I did not know what was wrong, but I felt uncomfortable all morning. Suddenly I had an urge to attend the 1st service and then visit my brother-in-law. I obeyed that voice. When I went to see my brother-in-law who had been ill for a long time, he was standing in the presence of death. I continuously prayed for him and sang praises right next to him. I helped him until he got the assurance of salvation. God sent me in order to save him, just one more soul.

This is a voice of the Holy Spirit, who makes you feel uncomfortable and urges you to do something.

The third one is the voice that speaks to you through messages.

In the Bible God says, 'do' or 'don't do.' God gives you peace when you follow as He advises you to do.

The voice of the Holy Spirit that most Christians hear is very gentle. If you do not ignore the voice coming into your heart but obey it, you will become very spiritual and be able to hear the voice clearly.

The voice of God Himself

There are several instances in the Bible that God speaks directly to people.

> *"Then the LORD came and stood and called as at other times, 'Samuel! Samuel!' And Samuel said, 'Speak, for Your servant is listening.' The LORD said to Samuel, 'Behold, I am about to do a thing in Israel at which both ears of everyone who hears it will tingle'"* (1 Samuel 3:10-11).

"And he fell to the ground and heard a voice saying to him, 'Saul, Saul, why are you persecuting Me?' And he said, 'Who are You, Lord?' And He said, 'I am Jesus whom you are persecuting'" (Acts 9:4-5).

The voice of God when He called me to be His servant was like a human voice but like clear water. It was clear but loud enough to make me tremble. It is impossible to describe how happy I was at that moment. It is very rare to hear the voice of God directly.

The voice of God, given through angel or man

"The angel said to the women, 'Do not be afraid; for I know that you are looking for Jesus who has been crucified'" (Matthew 28:5).

In the Bible we can find many occasions when God reveals His purposes through angels who are spirits serving God. Angels' voices are very beautiful.

God sometimes accomplishes His will through the mouth of man. He directs someone to talk to let us know that we should follow the truth or to let us feel what we should do to accomplish His plan. Therefore we must consider that God often talks to us through His servants, parish leaders, local area leaders, church members or children. We even see that God used a donkey to talk to Balaam in Numbers 22:28-30.

The voice of God given through prophecy

Prophecy is made by divine inspiration to show what will come to pass in the future. In the Bible there are many prophecies, which are fulfilled as stated.

"As we were staying there for some days, a prophet named Agabus came down from Judea. And coming to us, he took Paul's belt and bound his own feet and hands, and said, 'This is what the Holy Spirit says: "In this way the Jews at Jerusalem will bind the man who owns this belt and deliver him into the hands of the Gentiles"'" (Acts 21:10-11).

God gave many prophecies to me, His servant. I believe that every prophecy given to me has been accomplished or will be accomplished.

"Surely the LORD God does nothing unless He reveals His secret counsel to His servants the prophets. A lion has roared! Who will not fear? The LORD God has spoken! Who can but prophesy?" (Amos 3:7-8)

The voice of God given through revelation

Revelation is the utterance given through communication with God.

"The hand of the LORD was upon me, and He brought

me out by the Spirit of the LORD ... Again He said to me, 'Prophesy over these bones and say to them, 'O dry bones, hear the word of the LORD! Thus says the LORD GOD to these bones, "Behold, I will cause breath enter you that you may come to life. ... So I prophesied as I was commanded. and as I prophesied, ..." (Ezekiel 37:4-7)

To have a prophet is a wonderful blessing because we can get many revelations from God.

"The Revelation of Jesus Christ, which God gave Him to show to His bond-servants, the things which must soon take place; and He sent and communicated it by His angel to His bond-servant John" (Revelation 1:1).

I believed in every statement written in the Bible just as it is. So I asked God, while I was fasting 40 days with the hope for being fully armed with the word, to send me a prophet like Ezekiel, who would tell me what would take place in the future.

God remembered that I had prayed to Him with all my heart, loving Him with the hope to fully comprehend the difficult biblical verses. He answered my prayers.

In May 1982, God revealed to me I would start a church on a sizzling hot day, and it took place on July 25th just as God had told. Since this date God started to show His wonderful works through revelation just as He did through Ezekiel. A crippled man began to walk and jump because God gave strength to his tendons. Many miraculous healings came after this. Our church members' faith grew day by day. A lot of them met God and were born-again through His prophetic words.

From May 1983, God spoke to me and explained the difficult biblical verses. Those prophetic explanations were given through many fastings, overnight prayers and seven years of perseverance with crying out. His explanations answered all of my questions and gave me clear understanding of difficult verses.

I have mentioned totally five types of the voice of God. The other ways we can hear the voice of God are through individual dreams, visions and biblical verses. Individual dreams can be classified into three categories : no meaningful dreams, dreams of the spirit, and dreams of revelation through the Holy Spirit. To interpret the dreams requires a special discerning ability.

Matthew 11:27 says, *"All things have been handed over to Me by My Father; and no one knows the Son except the Father; nor does anyone know the Father except the Son, and anyone to whom the Son wills to reveal Him."* We need to receive the revelation to know our Father God. Revelation is given through communication with God, and we can hear the voice of God through communication.

As children of God, we can clearly understand the will of God through revelation so that we can obey God, who wants to make us good Christians who receive true blessings.

The Sovereign

I stopped leading revivals at other churches

In May 1983, God told me not to lead revivals at other churches any longer. Visiting churches to lead revivals, I was surprised to find these facts.

A lot of believers did not know exactly why Jesus was crucified and what the secret of the cross is : why you can be redeemed from your sins when you believe in Jesus Christ. They did not have full assurance of the living God. So God was the God of the dead, not of people who are still alive.

I really wanted to lead as many revival attendants as possible to salvation. The enemy Satan and the devil tried to interfere with my revival from the first day, Monday, while I preached about salvation, miracles, resurrection, the Second Advent of Jesus, and heaven. However, God gave me the final victory on Wednesday. I saw a lot of attendants, including pastors and ministers, cry and repent of their sins.

God revealed to me what topics I would preach at the revivals, and through prophecies He showed many attendants which way they must go. God showed us His love, grace and miraculous works at every revival I led. So many people met God and were changed. The crippled stood and walked, and various diseases of sick people were healed. Hallelujah!

However, God suddenly told me to stop leading those

revivals. He told me to receive His revelation of the word and to spread His perfect plans all over the world. He prophesied that the Jews would cry and repent of their sins in the near future.

Of course I obeyed Him, because I knew that I could not do anything but He could do everything, and because I believed that He wanted to perform His will through me, His servant. That is why I obeyed right away as He told me.

I devoted myself to the word of God and prayers

In May 1983 I started to prepare myself for receiving revelation. Every Sunday I left for the prayer mountain right after the worship service was over. That was to read the Bible, pray and receive revelation, Monday through Thursday. I was like John the apostle, who was confined on the island of Patmos and received revelation through communication with God. To receive revelation through communication with God, I had to put aside all church affairs including members' problems.

On Friday I came home to prepare for and preside over Friday overnight service. On Saturday I prayed for the sermons for the Sunday morning service and the evening service, made some home visitations, and counseled members.

God had me read the Bible carefully three times. And then He started to reveal to me, with full explanations, the difficult verses from Genesis to Revelation, including the topics which scientists or many scholars made objections on.

He had me read the Bible another three times. And He

explained to me the difficult verses and His purposes that I can help non-believers understand.

Additionally He had me read the Bible three times more. And He explained to me in detail about His Sovereignty over all creatures and the history of mankind. He also told me what He would do in the future.

To receive these revelations, I had to fight against the devil. My praying was like a bloody fight, just as Jesus did at Gethsemane until His sweat became like drops of blood falling to the ground or when Elijah prayed on the Mount of Carmel to receive fire from Heaven.

My weekdays' daily life started with the early morning prayer. Then I ate breakfast. After breakfast I prayed all morning to receive revelation. After lunch break I prayed, reading the Bible. If I had any wrong doing or a hidden sin in me, I could not go into the spiritual realm, so I could not receive revelation from God. To receive the revelations I had to win over the obstacles Satan brought, throw away every kind of evil, and be in peace with everyone, so that I would please God.

Through His revelations I experienced the miraculous power of God and His amazing love. I gave all glory and thanks to Him.

The Sovereign God

I sometimes look at a world map and dream of world mission. I can see the whole world on the map. The world looks quite small. I feel like I am looking at my palm. How would it look to God? When we look at our palms, we can see the detailed features of our palm, fingers and the big and small palm lines. We can tell the world would be like a palm to our Father. As we can move our palms on our own, God governs the world in His way.

God created all creatures from the first day to the sixth day and He set the world beautifully and made it adequate for mankind. Then lastly He created mankind and said to them, *"Be fruitful and multiply, and fill the earth, and subdue it"*(Genesis 1:28).

Then what does God reign?

First, God reigns over every creature in the universe.

He governs over the sun, the moon, stars in this world, other galactic systems and the whole universe in order, so that we have distinct day and night as well as four seasons. He governs over the sun, rain and all weather conditions.

Secondly, God reigns over the history of mankind.

They say the history of mankind is the combination of peace and war. In the Bible, human history including World War I, II, III, and ups and downs of the nations, is recorded exactly as they occurred or will occur. A lot of Christians, who have spiritually-opened eyes, realize that God governs over the history of mankind.

Thirdly, God reigns over all happenings in human life - life and death, fortune and misfortune of man.

He has the authority to govern life and death, although some people cut off their lives by themselves. No person can lengthen his or her span of life before death by himself (herself).

If someone's sin reaches its full measure, God takes his (her) life away from him (her). Oppositely, God sometimes extends the lifespan of a person as in the case of King Hezekiah in 2 Kings 20. God rewards us according to our deeds. His law is 'One reaps what he sows.' By this law God governs over life and death, fortune and misfortune of man, and the span of life. He does not preset the span of life for individuals.

If you sow righteousness, you will be blessed. If you sow evil, you will perish. The righteous, by faith, will be saved and receive the life in heaven. But the evildoers will be thrown into hell because the wages of sin is death. That is, God leads to heaven those who believe in Jesus Christ who is the way, the truth and the life, and to hell those who do not believe in Him. Likewise, God rewards evildoers with ruin and good-doers with heavenly blessings.

God gives the financial blessing to the hard workers, not to the lazy workers. If someone is righteous but lazy, he or she becomes poor. If evildoers dream of making a big fortune at one stroke, they eventually fail although they look temporarily successful.

God gives sunlight, air and rain to the evildoers as well as the righteous so that they both can live their lives in this world. At the same time God, as the Sovereign Lord governing over life and death, fortune and misfortune, rewards them according to their deeds.

Fourthly, God governs over everything in a way that the righteous who believe in Him will be prosperous, so it will go well with righteous people.

He is just, so He lets angels serve and guide His children according to the rule of the spiritual realm. He, knowing everything, gives blessings to His children when they ask Him in prayer. When His children pray, He sends angels to protect them from the devil, whereas non-believers cannot get protected from the devil or helped by angels.

In addition to this, the Holy Spirit, like the voice of God, leads believers. If you obey the voice of the Holy Spirit, you will be led to the safe and right way, not to the dangerous and wrong way. But non-believers cannot receive this blessing. This blessing is given to only those who love God.

I have met God, the Sovereign, who has given me abundant blessings. By His will I became His servant, who leads numerous people to the salvation and preaches His word.

I give all thanks to God, the Sovereign, who let me hear His voice to preach His word which is so perfect that until heaven and earth pass away, not the smallest letter or stroke of His word shall pass away.

The revelation

For three years after I accepted Jesus Christ, I went through perseverance. As a result, I threw away all of my sins and lived by the word of God. Then God gave me the gift of distinguishing between spirits. Since I received this gift, I came to feel uneasy when the word of God was misinterpreted by human thoughts or literal explanations.

As I stated above, I had three years of perseverance before I entered a theology school to be a servant of God as I was called. Among freshmen I was the student who asked questions to teachers most often. However, no teacher was able to answer my questions satisfactorily. So I stopped asking them and instead, from the second semester, I asked God directly to explain to me the difficult passages. Those passages did not go well with the word of God when they were literally interpreted. That is why I asked God to explain the spiritual meanings of them to me.

The revelation given through prophecies enables me to realize the spiritual meanings of the scriptures. How joyful it is! I cannot describe how much the Holy Spirit in me rejoices. The joy makes me forget how hard I exerted myself to receive revelation.

I'd like to introduce some sermon messages and prophecies given through revelation. These were gratefully shared with my church members and other church members as well as in cassette tapes of the sermons.

I give all thanks and glory to our Father God who has answered my prayers just as He promised in Jeremiah 33:3, *"Call to Me and I will answer you, and I will tell you great and mighty things, which you do not know."*

The parable of the wedding banquet (John 2:1-11)

I understand every one of you must have been to a wedding. The wedding is a holy and happy ceremony when a man and a woman become one flesh. However, the banquet that follows wedding ceremony is not always holy, because the attendants enjoy themselves drinking and eating.

Here, let's think about the first miracle that Jesus showed at the wedding banquet—changing water into wine.

Jesus came to the world to spread the gospel and revive the dead. Did He change the water into wine for people to enjoy drinking? Why did He show this miracle as the first one at starting His public ministry? I wondered why. So I earnestly prayed to God, who would let me know why Jesus did the miracle.

One day while I was earnestly praying to God to explain the parable of the wedding banquet to me, He spoke to me through the prophetess.

(Revelation is the utterance given through the prophet to reveal God's will. So the initial speaker is the Lord, and the prophet, who is filled with the Holy Spirit, utters. Please do not misunderstand revelation. Here in the revelations, 'I' indicates Jesus Christ.)

"Now I tell you My will through the prophetess.
What is the wedding banquet at Cana? Isn't it the first
miracle that I did, which was to change the water into

wine at the banquet?

My dear servant, I know I gave you one part, not the whole.

My dear servant, when you please Me and stand righteous, I will give you many messages explained. Be thankful.

My dear servant, I, using the power given by God, showed the first miracle at a wedding banquet in Cana. Why do you think I showed the first miracle at the wedding banquet?

The scripture says, 'People will be eating and drinking, marrying and giving in marriage, up to the day' (See Matthew 24:37-38).

Why was the flood brought at the time of Noah? I judged them with water, My word, because they were marrying, falling into debauchery and getting drunk.

Then, what does the Cana wedding banquet mean? Cana in Galilee means the world, the wedding banquet means marrying, and wine means drink. Drink will bring intoxication, intoxication will bring debauchery, and debauchery will lead them to fight. Then the banquet will show all wicked things in the world.

The scripture says that I, Jesus was invited to a wedding banquet. What did Satan do to Me after all? Did he not crucify Me? Everything was accomplished by His crucifixion. Therefore, inviting Me to the wedding banquet means inviting Me to crucifixion (See Matthew 26:50).

I had that written in the Bible so that you would know

the true meaning of it as well as the miracle that I did. This was written to show you the heart of God. When man reads it, he can only find a miracle. However, if you know My heart, you will receive the revelation as I want. No one knows the Father except the Son and anyone to whom the Son wills to reveal Him (See Matthew 11:27).

I tell you the truth, I showed this miracle so that the enemy Satan would be able to realize later that I would give eternal life to those who believe in Me by providing My blood as wine. The wine in the world makes people drunk, but the red color of the wine that I gave symbolizes My blood and it gives them eternal life.

I tell you the truth, when the enemy devill invited Me, I revealed to the people.

My dear servant! As the world invited Me, I was willingly crucified. The wine of the world made people drunk, but My wine was My blood that would give them eternal life. Only My Father and I knew about this. My dear servant, don't forget this significant meaning. Neither forget that the miracle was not done only by Myself.

My dear servant! Since I came to this world, all things have been done by faith. But I never made people believe something they had not seen. I always gave them revelation in faith. And God My Father blessed those who had faith to be overflowing with more faith.

When I said to Joseph, 'Don't be afraid to take Mary home as your wife,' he obeyed Me. When I said to Mary, 'you will give birth to a son,' she believed that as well. As they believed, the baby could be conceived by the Holy Spirit. Without faith, no miracle would have happened.

My dear servant! Nothing would have happened if it had not been for the glory of God and His providence. And without faith, nothing would have been done. God has done everything so justly that even the enemy Satan cannot accuse Him at all. I performed the miracle at the wedding banquet, because My mother of flesh had faith and she wanted Me to do this. You know that I cannot perform a miracle where there is no faith. Also the reason I raised Tabitha from death was to show you that God could do any miracle when He is pleased in His heart. I tell you the truth, I performed a big miracle in every village so that the news would spread to all places.
My dear servant! Be aware that I didn't perform many miracles in one place. Keep all of your understanding of what I have said to you."

Through this revelation, I came to understand the word of God with ease. Three days after Jesus began His public ministry, He and His disciples as well as Mary were invited to a wedding at Cana, Galilee. This is recorded in John 2. When the wine ran out, the mother of Jesus said to Him, *"They have no wine"* (v. 3). And Jesus said to her, *"Woman, what does that have to do with us? My hour has not yet come"* (v. 4). His mother trusted that Jesus would perform a miracle and told the servants to do whatever Jesus would tell them. Because of this faith, Jesus could perform the miracle.

Jesus said to the servants, *"Fill the waterpots with water."* (v. 7) So they filled them to the brim. Then Jesus told them, *"Draw some out now and take it to the headwaiter"* (v. 8) They did so and the master of the banquet tasted the water that had been turned into wine. He did not realize where it had come from but the servants who drew the water knew. Then he called the bridegroom aside and said. *"Every man serves the good wine first, and when the people have drunk freely, then he serves the poorer wine but you have kept the good wine until now"* (v. 10).

"This beginning of His signs Jesus did in Cana of Galilee, and manifested His glory, and His disciples believed in Him" (v. 11).

This verse compares the beginning and the end of the public ministry of Jesus to a wedding banquet.

Now let me explain this incident spiritually. Jesus being invited to the wedding symbolizes that the world invited Jesus to be crucified and he accepted and died on the cross. The wedding banquet refers to the last days when the world will be full of eating, drinking and sin. Turning water into wine stands for the blood of Jesus that He shed on the cross to give us eternal life.

The master's comment, "the wine was the best" symbolizes the joy, of those who have their sins forgiven by drinking the blood of Jesus, is the best because they have hope for the heavenly kingdom. Jesus revealed His glory by His crucifixion and by His resurrection three days after death, and He said that no sign would be given except the sign of the prophet Jonah (Matthew 12:39).

His disciples put their faith in Him after seeing His first miracle. This fact symbolizes that they truly believed Jesus and could risk their lives to preach the resurrection of Jesus Christ and the message of the cross only after they witnessed his crucifixion and resurrection. How disappointed God must be, if we understand the first miracle of Jesus merely as to celebrate a wedding banquet!

The miracle was symbolic of what Jesus was going to do to save mankind as He started His public ministry. I was so excited to understand this spiritual meaning. Even now, my heart gets full of joy when I look back on that time.

The fall and recovery of Israel (John 19:23-24)

God also revealed His will for Israel to me through the Holy Spirit:

"My dear servant! I was born as an Israelite, as a descendant of David. I tell you the truth, Israel is My body. As my body was hurt, the whole nation of Israel was hurt. Because the Israelites hurt their King, their country was damaged. As the spear pierced Me, Israel was to be pierced. As My clothes were divided, all the Israelites were to be scattered. As lots were cast for My undergarment, so the

Israelites would lose their country.

My dear servant! When you are united in one spirit and rejoice in Me without any evil in your heart, your Father can do all wonders and signs for you. But who can believe this? The reason I reveal this to you is because I want you to preach this to the Israelites. After you are taken up to heaven, all the Israelites will hear this and be moved in their hearts to repent of their sins. Be aware that I have not revealed this to you until you were free from sin.

What did the Israelites say when they crucified Me? They said, 'His blood shall be on us and on our children!' (Matthew 27:25) And your Father God let it happen just as they said.

My dear servant! Why was it recorded that My undergarment was seamless woven in one piece from top to bottom? It means that Israel has remained as a nation since Jacob's name was changed to Israel. If My undergarment was torn, could Israel stand again? Therefore My undergarment must remain one piece as it means that Israel would be reformed.

My dear servant! Even though the Israelites were scattered all over the world as my clothes were torn into four pieces, their hearts remained the same toward God as My undergarment was not torn by the soldiers."

Now I will explain in detail the spiritual meaning of the above. As the Roman soldiers crucified Jesus and tore His clothes into four pieces, the Israelites, after they crucified Jesus, were scattered in four directions when the Romans conquered them in 70 AD.

The soldiers took His undergarment, too. But as it was seamless, woven in one piece from top to bottom, the soldiers cast lots instead of tearing it. This means that no

orce could stop the spirit of the Israelites, who respected and feared God and loved their country since Jacob.

And as it was written, Israel was actually reformed on May 14, 1948 (See the Book of Ezekiel 38). The fact that the nation was reformed about 2,000 years after it had been destroyed thoroughly by Titus in 70 AD is a miracle of miracles, which can happen only by the will of God.

6

PRECIOUS LIFE

Recollection

My body was wet all over with sweat, but my heart was jumping for joy. 'Where can I hear these precious words? Who can teach me the wonderful word of God?' My heart was pounding, and my eyes were full of hot tears.

'The secrets of the clothes and garments of Jesus, the prophecy of the fall and restoration of Israel...'

I could not stop thanking God who had revealed His precious words to me. I kept all of the revelations in my heart. I thought over this mysterious work of God. Why does He do this for me? The hot tears of my eyes for His deep love for me were responding to this question.

After I received the amazing revelation from God

I believe my life was completely led by the will of God

according to His plan. I cherish my life because it has been blessed up to now with miracles and trials at all times.

I was a common man, introspective, stubborn and small of body. Why did God call me as His servant, to guide numerous people to salvation these last days? Why did He select me to have such a big dream of world evangelization? Why had He led me and watched over my life so far? I could not get a clear answer alone. I was merely a common man, who had nothing better than other men. If I had something different, it was my heart. My heart was faithful, seeking righteousness, and of long endurance.

God chose David to be a king not because of his outward appearance but because of his heart. Likewise, God chose me to spread the good news all over the world, not because of my appearance but because of my heart. I could not help but thank Him for the choice He made in me with love.

From the time He chose me, He had me go through all kinds of trials. Reflecting on those trials, I whole-heartedly thank God. Unless I had been refined through those trials, I could not have become what I am, His precious beloved servant.

God told Abraham to offer Isaac. He let Jacob wrestle with a man until the man wrenched the socket of his hip. And He disciplined me until I put away every kind of evil.

When I became a new Christian, God had me struggle severely to live according to the word. While I was a deacon, He endowed me with strength so that I could keep all His commandments.

God said, *"You have heard that it was said, 'You shall not commit adultery'; but I say to you that everyone who looks at a woman with lust for her has already committed adultery with her in his heart"* (Matthew 5: 27-28). To cultivate this message I fasted and prayed for three years, and I was able to overcome adultery.

God's discipline did not end there. While I was studying at theology school and preparing for starting a church, God had me block my own thoughts and let me act with the inspiration of the Holy Spirit in my heart. I no longer had my own thoughts and will but the heart of the Lord.

Before I started a church, I often became a target of unfavorable criticism. Even though some Christians regarded me as a heretic or trials came upon me, I always kept the same attitude. I loved the people who gave me a hard time. I prayed and thanked God for them. That is because God had refined me. This is why God blessed my new church and increased the members daily so that I could guide many people to salvation.

Even after our church grew and was settled, I was continuously disciplined under the hand of God. His discipline made me not only throw away every kind of evil so that I pleased Him, but also be at peace with everyone. He helped me to cultivate those desirable attributes that a pastor would need to work at a big church in the future. It is because my church would produce a large number of servants for God, and would be a shelter where many believers could rest.

How considerate God's love is! He protected our church from accusations of the enemy. He wanted our church to receive only blessings. If there was any quarrel or jealousy in the church, God stopped giving us blessings and gave no revelation to me either.

I was to be the shepherd who washes the feet of others just as Jesus did for His disciples. I was not to lose any of the souls that God sent to me. I was to willingly carry the cross just as Jesus did to save others, and accomplish the assignment given to me by God, despite any disgrace or shame.

Every day started and ended with many tears. Thinking of my church members, I spent my days praying for them in tears. I put up a tearful petition to God for His revelation. And I asked God to take good care of my church and my congregation.

One day God gave me this magnificent gift of a song called, 'My dear servant.' It was His love and comfort that nobody else could give to me. The Lord composed the words of this song.

With My blood I wiped away all your sins.
Now I give life to the dead
With My power through you.
I will always be with you.

I made a covenant through My body and blood.
My dear servant, believe Me.
Be bold wherever you go,

For I am the power of your life.
I am the power of your true life.
Hold Me and win the victory.
My dear servant, keep going forward.
I will always be with you.

Oh, Father! Receive them!
Receive My beloved servant!
As My Father trusted Me and sent Me down,
I will also trust you.

You are My power and My love.
My dear servant,
When you meet Me as I come in the light of glory,
I will rejoice to see you.

After I was ordained as a pastor

I was ordained as a pastor four years after I started my church. It was a joyful event for all of my church members. I was moved to tears to see the love they had for me.

After the ordination, God urged me to fast and pray for twenty-one days, following the example of Daniel. I left my church and congregation as God guided. He urged me to take the first step as a pastor, communicating with Him and receiving prophecies of revelation.

During the twenty-one days of fasting and prayer, I missed my church members very much. At the same time I realized again how precious they were to me.

How has God brought my congregation since the beginning of the church! God made every member experience the living God. God worked on them to feel and experience that He is the living God. Paralytics stood up and walked. Those who were seriously injured by traffic accidents also walked and leaped. God blessed us with so many miraculous works. Accordingly, the faith of my congregation grew day by day. And many people came, met, and experienced God. As Paul confessed in his letter to the Corinthians, *"I became your father through the gospel"* (1Corinthians 4:15). my congregation was precious to me.

From the beginning of my ministry, God helped me to preach to my congregation the message of faith. So my congregation could plant confidence and faith in their heart that they could do anything with God's help.

Through the message of hope, God helped my congregation to obtain the assurance of salvation and resurrection, so that they came to have the hope of heaven. God helped my entire congregation to struggle against their sins to throw them away and take the victory over the world as citizens of heaven.

And through the message of love, God helped my congregation to adopt the heart of Jesus Christ and to live a holy life so that they bore blessed fruits in their lives. He raised my church members to work hard even to the point of death for His kingdom, to rise and shine. He blessed them to be great workers for the church, accomplishing many assignments so that they would get rewards in heaven.

I thanked God once again for each member of my congregation. I prayed for them to receive more blessings.

"Oh, my Father! Thank You for giving me this congregation. The entire members - elders, senior and junior deacons and deaconesses, young adults and students - all believe that You are living. And they live a faithful life. Father, thank You so much for giving this precious congregation to me!"

Now we are filled with the Holy Spirit and grace. We are one in love, like the early churches. I believe we will be like the church in Philadelphia that God praised. My church members, who try to live according to the word of God, fighting against the sins to the point of shedding blood, appreciate my advices and obey what I teach. How thankful this is!

None of these would have been possible if God had not guided us. I would have had none of these church members if God had not sent them. I can't help thanking God who will always guide me until the end of the world.

I did not realize that my hot tears of gratitude were streaming down my face onto the pillow. My chest was swollen with joy. My mind was racing back to days past.

My past

When God called me as His servant in May 1978, I was a thirty-six-year-old man and a father of three daughters. I was not able to remember much of my past. I could not remember what I had learned in school.

I was not the kind of person that would go to a college to study theology. To make matters worse, to preach in front of many people seemed absolutely impossible. This is why I could not immediately obey what God commanded me. However, He knew that my heart was willing to obey. So He called me to be His servant and I eventually obeyed Him.

Jesus said in Mark 9:23, *" 'If You can?' All things are possible to him who believes."*

I asked God, who knew everything about me and what I needed. So I put everything in Him, and I relied on Him alone.

I had lived my life in my own way

Once I realized that God had led my life from birth to the time when I met Jesus, I came to cherish my past.

I did not know anything about God. I would not admit that God exists. I did not care where I was from, where I would go, and what I should live for. I just lived my life in my own way. I had no hope or value in my life. This was my past life. Because of my past life, my present life would look far more valuable to me.

When I was in my pre-teen years growing up in my hometown, I dreamed of a great future: an intellectual, classy and rich one. I was quite affected by my rigid father, a scholar of Chinese classics. I believe God had me grow with the basic human aptitude under my father's discipline.

When I took the entrance exam for the junior high school, I saw how much man could deceive other men. During my middle school days when I stayed at my cousin brother's house, I experienced some hardships in my life. I was a born optimist. But a bad-looking tooth on one side made me a shy person. I became quiet and self-conscious so that I never asked for help although I was in need. This self-centeredness strengthened my endurance and taught me how to handle hardships.

My high school days in Seoul taught me how to look toward the future by myself, with no one's help. I became very independent. I could see the inward workings of man. But at the same time, when I perceived the inward workings of those whom I respected, I felt something like vanity in life.

To go to college I had to study for two years because I failed in the entrance exam when I was a senior at high school. I lost my ability to remember what I studied, so I tried to commit suicide. How bad this was! If you do not know why and for what reason you live, it is very tragic. I thought my life had no value in this world. I decided to die rather than to live a tragic life. I thought dying would get rid of all problems and pains. But I realized that I could not control my own life, but I found someone else could. It was God who made me realize this.

Since that time, my miraculous survival continued.

I took twenty sleeping pills, but I survived. They say two 720-ml bottles of whisky are strong enough to kill a healthy man. I drank five bottles, but I did not die. Now I know why. But I didn't know that only God controlled my life and death.

After I entered a college, I was never interested in studying. Besides, too many demonstrations made me sick of my school life. So I joined the army.

While I was serving in the army, I came to know a lady through a pen pal program. My military life was fun because of my female pen pal's letters. We kept corresponding with each other until I finished my military duty, and we got married. Our relationship moved too quickly. But having no experience dating girls, I did not know what else I should do.

I was a baby in my adult life, knowing almost nothing of the world. I thought I could do everything by myself as I studied and dreamed. I thought I would accomplish my manly life as I wanted to live by my will. I was sure that I would cultivate a successful life with my own wisdom.

I had a dream. So I visited my parents with my detailed plan.

"Mother, father, please listen to me carefully. If you give me my portion of your inheritance in advance, my wife can open a beauty shop and I can go back to college and go abroad to study. Look at this plan, please."

Showing them mathematical accounting numbers including annual interests, I kept asking them for twenty days. Finally I won. I was so happy on the way back to Seoul with the money of inheritance.

Right soon I was tempted. My elder sister suggested an idea that could help me make some profit by lending my money until I would use it to open my wife's beauty shop. She was my trustful sister, so I handed all of my money over to her.

A few months later, I could not get any money back, even

interest. My wife, who promised to pay back the money (she borrowed from me) for my tuition soon, spent it away. Neither could I go abroad to study, nor register for my college courses in my country. My parents, who gave me money because of my earnest request, took the attitude - it's not our business.

I woke up to find myself penniless. In my mind success seemed so simple, but the reality was dreadful. Until all the money I inherited was swindled, I thought my dream would come true. However, my dream came crashing down. My dream of my happy marriage life was broken off. Therefore my marriage was a miserable one. The last dream remained in me, this was to get a job, attend and complete an evening college, and be the head of a family in a sweet and peaceful home.

'Although my life looks common and ordinary, if I overcome all of these obstacles, my life will be meaningful.' When I made up my mind to live with my best efforts, I began to feel some happiness.

Soon after I got a job, I had to quit it because I fell sick due to excessive drinking. I could not hear any sound, and my weak body was streamed with cold sweat. I could not even do the easiest work.

Since I was jobless, making no money, I became isolated from the community. My wife's love for me gradually cooled. My parents' love and my brothers' love also cooled. Even my wife's family called me, 'Crippled brother-in-law' or 'Cheater.'

As I had a miserable past

As I think back on my past days of sickness, I realize they were another precious time of mine. How miserably poor I was! I could not afford the hospital treatment, so I had to stay home for several years. I had to live my life on the money my wife borrowed under the condition that we would pay it back including daily interest, which was excessively high.

Because of this sore experience I came to feel mercy for poor people, and I often willingly provided financial support to them afterwards.

Deep in my heart I came to realize that human love changes, but the love of God, who healed me completely, does not. I thanked Him for His love and I came to love God with all my strength, with all my heart, and with all my life.

The long wasteful time of my sick days made me not only understand the painful heart of sick people, but also cherish the time given to me. So I worked as hard as possible, much harder than the others.

My past had no direction. I was afloat on a river. So I came to follow Jesus who is the way and the truth and the life.

Moreover, as I had failed to make my own plans come true for myself, I then left my life totally to God so that I could live a victorious life. In the past, I was a man of narrow thinking, living only for money, honor and social reputation. As a result, I obtained no satisfaction, just disappointment, not joy but sorrow, and not peace but only grief.

The painful life of my past helped me to meet God who is living, and to realize how deep and merciful His love is. That is why I regard my past as precious.

My present

God, who is merciful, knocked on the door of my heart several times. However, I was too ignorant, foolish and stubborn to open my heart toward Him, so I had to suffer from failure, disappointment and grief.

One day Jesus, who is the way and the truth and the life, came to me through my humble elder sister. Although I involuntarily showed up before God through my elder sister's earnest request, Jesus warmly treated me and gave me many gifts.

"I tell you that in the same way, there will be more joy in heaven over one sinner who repents than over ninety-nine righteous persons who need no repentance" (Luke 15:7).

Only the Lord Jesus, always the Lord Jesus

I was 100% changed. 'Can I ever get back any of those lost seven years while I was sick to the point of death? What can I learn from them?'

When I drew a mental picture of my future, I felt something like power rising in me. Unknowingly I clenched my fists. 'Now God loves me. Then nothing will be a problem for me. I know God is living and almighty.' I felt peace from the bottom of my heart.

'Only Jesus, always Jesus' was becoming my motto for my new life. Like Saul who met Jesus on the road to Damascus, I was suddenly changed at the very moment of meeting God.

I believed that God could restore anyone who was dying, so I left all of my life to Him. When I found any sins in me, I immediately threw them away, including my worldly pleasures. I quit drinking and playing Badook (a game playing with white and black rock to make territory) and Hwatoo (a Korean card game).

I found joy only in fasting, praying, reading and studying the Bible, and cultivating the word of God in my heart. This was my regular daily life.

God gave me a heavy laborious job to restore my health while cultivating endurance. I could recognize well what environment the laborers lived under and what was their way of thinking. So I was able to evangelize to them, giving my testimony.

God also led me to manage a bookstore, where I realized that if I did business remaining in the truth of God, He blessed me abundantly. While gaining wisdom and experience to run the store, I could also evangelize to many customers there. That was God's way of training and making me a good worker who could guide many souls to salvation.

God helped me to throw away my sins and live by His word. He gave me a fierce love with which I would evangelize to many souls. When I prayed with faith in His love for people, God showed His miraculous power through me in various ways. Sick people were healed as I prayed for them. My second daughter was hit by a car and taken to the hospital. She was in coma. I brought her home and prayed all night for her in faith. And I left her life in God's hands. Because I had faith in God who is almighty, I knew that God could cure my daughter. I had no doubt of it at all. God completely cured my daughter faster than the medical doctors ever could.

Before she was healed, our neighbors jeered at us. "They are strange Christians." "Why don't they take the girl to the hospital?"

But later on, they came to believe in God, giving glory to Him. Hallelujah!

My first daughter who had a very bad skin disease and my third daughter who had a concussion of the brain were also healed completely through prayers. None of my family has gone to see a doctor since we believed in Jesus. We did not need medicine but God's power to be cured. We gave all the glory to God.

My family really liked to give offerings to God. We experienced that God blesses people to reap what they sow, so we gave Him as much as we could.

My house was always full of the sounds of praise and praying. So, we could effectively evangelize to many of those who simply listened.

"What makes you so happy every day?" They often asked

us.

"You will also be happy and joyful if you believe in Jesus."

Our house was always bustling with visitors. My wife, who is a good cook, liked to cook and serve them with her delicious food. My wife and her cell members kept praying, praising, reading the Bible and having fellowship. As a result, the number of her cell members increased up to seven times. This rapid growth taught us that love and prayers are essential for inviting the miracles of God.

Arise, shine

God continually showed us His miracles since we started our church. Even when nothing was visible, God answered our prayers, as we believed in Him.

"Though your beginning was insignificant, Yet your end will increase greatly" (Job 8:7).

"Arise, shine; for your light has come, And the glory of the LORD has risen upon you. For behold, darkness will cover the earth And deep darkness the peoples; But the LORD will rise upon you And His glory will appear upon you. Nations will come to your light, And kings to the brightness of your rising" (Isaiah 60:1-3).

We were nine in all when we started the church. Then God sent us many new members, some from far away and some close by. He raised them to be good leaders or ministers. Since the first day we started our church, He led us to pray for world mission. And He gave me a vision of going overseas to lead crusades, showing miraculous signs and wonders.

He gave me a great vision. Although we had no chairs to sit on and the room space was smaller than 900 square feet, we prayed for world mission from the very first day. Nonbelievers might have laughed at us. However, our members rapidly increased with newcomers week by week, and their faith also rapidly grew.

Since I started my church, I have stood on the front to spread the gospel, supporting other starting churches that were in financial need.

For now hundreds of pastors and ministers are running to save souls, and all of my church members are praying to be good workers who may please God. To evangelize the whole nation we have built local sanctuaries in and around Seoul and branch churches in the other provincial areas in our country. And we have established many overseas branch churches all over the world to spread the gospel as much as we can.

Thankfully many ministers God are growing spiritually, and a lot of members are working hard for the kingdom of God with their God-given talents. I believe these ministers of God and members will be changed spiritually so that they will play more powerful and significant roles in world mission. How wonderful it will be! Every day I earnestly pray for the vision God gave me. I hope it may come true as early as possible.

God wants us to have prosperous future, guide millions

and millions of people to salvation, and rise and shine to accomplish God's purposes. God also wants me to spread the word on behalf of the Lord and perform more miracles than Jesus did in this world.

I hoped that God might explain the difficult biblical passages directly to me. I fasted and prayed for this hope for seven years. Finally God answered my prayers. How joyful it was! He explained the difficult passages to me. I have already received revelations of Genesis, Exodus, Leviticus, Job, the Four Gospels, 1 & 2 Corinthians, Hebrews, 1 John, Revelation and other important scriptures. I'm still receiving revelations of the rest of the scriptures. The revelation of heaven alone covers more than 100 pages on college notebooks. I'm planning to publish it later at the proper time. The readers, if they love God, will feel the Holy Spirit in them jumping for joy.

God still urges me to exert myself in praying and getting armed with the word so that I may show the power of God. I really want to visit every member of my church to have fellowship and intimacy. I hope all of my members understand why I cannot do that.

I know the Last Day is near. That is why I use my time these days as sparingly as possible. Although I am doing my best to accomplish God's will, I feel some shortage.

I remember God said to me, *"My dear servant, if you feed your flock in a good pasture, everyone of them will be lifted up at the last hour."*

As Jesus did in this world, I would like to live a holy life to be a good shepherd who guides dying people to salvation. I believe that to be a good shepherd, I must exert all my abilities for preparing messages and performing all my pastoral duties. Then God will say that I am a good shepherd, my members are good flock of sheep, and my church is a good church. So today I am also devoting myself to praying, preaching and utilizing God's power. With this devotion of mine I could guide a great number of people to salvation, and I will guide more and more from now on to glorify God.

After I met Jesus, my life became more valuable, meaningful and joyful than that of before. How delightful and hopeful my life is! I can't help but thank God.

My future

"My dear servant who I had chosen before time began! If you get yourself armed with the word for three years, I will let you cross over rivers and seas to show miraculous signs and wonders."

God never fails to keep what He says. He kept His word. When I finished three years of studying the word, He guided me to hold a revival for the first time. After this, I have held many revivals. Through the revival meetings I came to realize that it is very hard to see true faith in people.

You will show miraculous signs and wonders

At first I wondered why God chose me in these last days to do the world mission. I came to know why. There are many ministers who are preaching the word. How many of them would live by the word so that God uses them for His purposes?

When God called me, I was not qualified for being His servant. So I had to do so many overnight prayers and fast for God's help. I firmly believed that God would help me because I had experienced God's almighty power.

I was comparatively old. I had poor memory. So, without God's help I could not study theology at school or do any pastoral job. Therefore my prayers were deeply earnest from the bottom of my heart. Gratefully, God answered my prayers like fire. I did not have to try to remember anything with my brain. The Holy Spirit in me guided and instructed me. If God wanted, it remained in my heart. If not, I forgot right away. The events of my past life were forgotten, but the word of God was kept in my heart. I received clear inspiration, not human thoughts. I came to have the power of God, receiving revelation through clear inspiration.

For now, I have almost finished getting armed with the word through revelations. It is time for me to shine, so the whole world may see God's power.

There are so many people who are wrongfully taught the word. A lot of people are wandering because they do not know about the word and the will of God. There are many people who do not live according to what God wants them to do because they do not know it. Many believers have dead faith. All these are chaff. They verbally say, 'I believe in God.'

But they do not believe in their heart. That is why they will go to hell.

"His winnowing fork is in His hand, and He will thoroughly clear His threshing floor; and He will gather His wheat into the barn, but He will burn up the chaff with unquenchable fire" (Matthew 3:12).

They do not know how terrible hell is and how unquenchable the fire of the hell is. God of love, who has patiently waited for the chaff to be changed, gave me the powerful words to preach to them. As I have mentioned before, I do not tell them just to believe in Jesus Christ, but I teach them why they get saved if they believe in Jesus Christ. I explain the message of the cross in easy terms to understand. Then they have faith to be saved, growing as the wheat, not the chaff.

God talked to me about the Second Advent of Christ and the Rapture. He told me it is very near. He talked to me about where in heaven I will be, what kind of rewards I will receive, and what crowns I will wear in heaven.

Through His explanations I came to know what a glorious life I will live in heaven, so I decided to work as hard as possible, giving everything, even my life for the salvation of people. I know how Jesus' disciples died. One of them was thrown into a pot of boiling oil, one was cut in half with a saw, and another one was hung upside down on a cross. But all of them were thankful for their death, praised God, and rejoiced. I will do whatever it takes to extend the kingdom of God and to save people.

My three missions

My first mission God assigned is the world mission. I remind myself of this every day. As God has guided us, we have sent missionaries domestically and internationally as many as possible. At the same time we have established branch churches to guide people to salvation. We also have spread the gospel at home and abroad by radio, TV, newspapers, videotapes and books.

To think of world mission makes me very happy. I see what God told us come true, continuously praying by faith. He said to me, "You will do wonders and miraculous signs, crossing over the mountains and the seas." He is accomplishing the world mission through my church.

My second mission is to change the people into the wheat, not the chaff. I believe that God will help my sheep not to have dead faith but to have living faith to be the wheat, living by the word and accomplishing their duties.

While I was a new Christian, no one explained to me in detail how to pray or what the message of the cross is. So I could not tell which way to go to find true faith. I prayed for a long time to find the quickest way to a deep faith. Since I found the quickest way, I have given a full explanation to my congregation.

For example, "To pray, you must kneel down, open your mouth widely to speak aloud, and call on God with all your heart."

"The order of powerful prayer is to pray with a thankful heart first, to repent, and to ask God to cast away the devil, and then to ask God for your own needs. If you pray for His kingdom and His righteousness first and then for your personal needs, God will answer your prayers abundantly."

"Therefore I say to you, all things for which you pray and ask, believe that you have received them, and they will be granted you" (Mark 11:24).

To teach on how to pray is just one topic. I have taught my congregation step by step in detail to help them live according to the word, because the word is alive and powerful so as to change the people from chaff to wheat. To get the people of chaff changed to the people of wheat is my primary mission, so a long time ago I made a detailed plan.

'Father, I want to be the servant who reaps the greatest harvest. It has not been a long time since you called me, but please help me to be the leader whose harvest is the greatest.'

My third mission is to guide my congregation as the faithful grain to prepare themselves as brides beautifully dressed for the husband.

The grains are the believers who are reborn by water and the Holy Spirit and live by the word of God. Normally new Christians feel uneasy about following the word of God. But if they exert themselves to pray and follow the word exactly as they hear it, they can eventually practice it in their deeds.

Then they can bear the fruits of light, righteousness, and the Holy Spirit. When they succeed to cultivate love, they become filled with the word and prayers, being ready for the Lord's coming.

"Be on the alert then, for you do not know the day nor the hour" (Matthew 25:13).

The five wise virgins took oil in jars along with their lamps. The five foolish ones, however, took their lamps but did not take enough oil with them. So the foolish ones could not meet the bridegroom (Mathew 25:1-13).

We must not be the foolish ones, but be the wise ones who are waiting for the Lord to come again. We must be the ones who rise and meet the Lord when He comes down from heaven with a loud command, with the voice of the archangel, and with the trumpet call of God. The dead in Christ will rise first, and then we who are still alive and are left will be caught up together with them in the clouds to meet the Lord in the air. We must complete the preparation as the bride beautifully dressed for the husband on time.

How joyful will it be when the Lord comes down in the air? How happy will we be? We will lay down all of our worldly burdens and meet our everlasting bridegroom, the Lord. How wonderful it will be! However, if you do not wake up, He will come like a thief. If you are alert and self-controlled, He won't come to you like a thief.

We, as the grain, bearing good fruits and playing the roles

of light and salt in the world, will be awake when we meet the Lord. We'll be joyfully praising when we meet our bridegroom, the Lord!

"Come, Lord Jesus." (Revelation 22:20)

Looking forward to the day, I will work harder and harder to save more people with the vision of world mission. While I work for world mission, the people who listen to the messages that I preach will turn into the grain, living by the word and praying continually, so that they will be awake to meet the Lord when He comes again. I believe the day is very near, right in front of our face. I give many thanks to God for this great joy.

We can work for His kingdom and His righteousness far more than at other times because we know we were born in the last days. Besides, we'll be lifted up alive in the air. How wonderful this blessing is!

Thanks for everything

"God is not a man, that He should lie, nor a son of man, that He should repent; Has He said, and will He not do it? Or has He spoken, and will He not make it good?" (Numbers 23:19)

God has blessed me as fully as He promised. I give all

thanks to God.

God said to Simon Bar-jonah, who was a fisherman, in Matthew 16:18-19, *"I also say to you that you are Peter, and upon this rock I will build My church; and the gates of Hades will not overpower it. I will give you the keys of the kingdom of heaven; and whatever you bind on earth shall have been bound in heaven, and whatever you loose on earth shall have been loosed in heaven."*

God chose me, merely a humble man, before time began and brought me into this world during the last days before our Lord comes again. He showed His miraculous power in my body so that I came to have strong faith from the start. How thankful and how wise His work is! I recognized His wisdom, although I was too ignorant to understand His significant plan.

After God gave me the faith, He has answered all of my prayers, guiding and giving me victory and joy through all trials and difficulties.

I thank God for guiding me as His servant to accomplish His great plans with His power. He gave me the vision of the world mission, and sent me a lot of members. He has so loved my congregation that He changed them into the grain. I feel a deep gratitude for His love.

My second eldest sister guided me to get true life. I owe her my life. I was too ignorant to know God is living. But I esteemed myself wise enough, so I ignored my elder sister. She never gave up evangelizing to me. She kept praying earnestly to God. Without her tearful and earnest prayers and fasting for long days and nights over my soul and sick body, I would not be what I am today. She continuously talked to me, "Brother, once you go to church, God will heal all of your sickness and you will meet Him." I believe only her faithful prayers brought the miracle to me.

"Oh, Father God! Your blessing on me is overflowing. Where and what would I have been doing if my sister hadn't helped me to accept Jesus? I cannot imagine how dreadful it would be. If I had ignored the love of God or hadn't believed in the Lord, I would have ended up going to hell."

My elder sister is now serving me as her shepherd like she serves the Lord. She is still praying for me all the time. I cannot express the deep gratitude I feel for her. I thank my elder sister again for guiding me to salvation.

Here, I'd like to thank my family members (my parents, brothers, sisters and relatives) and neighbors. They helped me as much as they could. My parents raised me with love, and my siblings loved and supported me in many ways. My family members supported me when I needed food, clothes, and place to live. My neighbors helped me to solve my problems. And my friends helped me to get a job and start a new life. I thank every one of these people. Because of their love and help, I could feel the love and the will of God for me.

I thank Rev. Younghoon Yi, who counseled and advised me when I began to live a new changed life after I met God. I also thank the Christian families who led me selflessly when I was a beginner, professor-pastors who taught me at the theology school after God called me, my classmates who studied together with me, and the seniors and juniors at the school of theology.

Here I have one more person I cherish and must thank. She has been with me sharing all of my sorrow and grief. She is my wife, Boknim Lee, who is now working as the President of the Manmin Prayer Center. She cries out to God day and night all the time.

The happiness of the wife depends upon the husband. Unfortunately my wife had to spend seven years of suffering while nursing me, her husband, who got sick right after we married. She had to work to earn money for our family. I can only imagine how sorrowful her life was, taking care of the family as a young woman. However, in spite of living in poverty, she came to be thankful for everything after she met Jesus. She thanked and prayed earnestly for whatever trials came against us.

Unless she took care of me, sacrificing her life, I couldn't have studied to be a servant of God. She relied only on the almighty God with faith, helping me along the way. She still prays for me for long hours every day.

I sincerely thank my wife for her hard work, endurance and prayers.

I feel a deep gratitude for those who were with me when starting our church. Sometimes I rebuke them because I love them so much. They are in my heart as my cherishing assets, who obeyed the will of God to establish our Manmin Central

Church.

Just as God appointed Aaron and Hur to help Moses, He gave me great members who prayed together with me. All of them became one in praying with all their heart. Then God answered our prayers case by case promptly. He often revealed His glory so that we could guide many people to salvation. He gave us tremendous growth and multiplied the numbers in my congregation because our church was standing firmly on the foundation.

God sent me a lot of people, including faithful prayer warriors who would assist me in getting armed with God's revelation and in cultivating my pastoral vessel to be big enough for many more souls to come and find rest. He chose those devoted prayer warriors, being obedient to the point of death, who would pray for His kingdom and His righteousness with all their strength, with all their heart, with all their mind, and with all their soul.

Those devoted prayer warriors come to church and pray in one spirit every day. They gather in the Prayer House at 10 o'clock in the morning and pray for the physically and mentally sick. And after lunch they have another prayer meeting.

"Where does your mom go every day?"
"She goes to church."
"Don't the Christians go to church only on Sundays?"
"My church holds prayer meetings every day. That's why my mom goes every day."
"Oh, your church does..."

A teacher asked her student why his mother always goes out. But the teacher couldn't understand why his mother goes to church every day.

These devoted prayer warriors are soldiers of the cross who have met God. So, to return His love they devote themselves to praying every day, receiving no pay of course. How lovely they are! I thank all those devoted prayer warriors, who only look forward to rewards of heaven and work for the church with all their strength.

No matter how hard the shepherd may work, the miraculous work of God does not appear unless the congregation obeys their shepherd.

God has sent many people to Manmin Joong-ang Church. God chose every one of them according to His special plan, so through trials He changes them into righteous men and women of God. Most of the elders, senior deaconesses, deacons and other members love God so much that they are struggling against sins to the point of shedding blood to live by His word. They believe in the almighty God, so they live by faith, working hard with all their strength and obeying me to the point of death.

It is very rare to see believers with true faith. My congregation, however, are living by faith, rejoicing for hope, and loving each other. I love and thank my entire congregation, especially the leaders who pray more than three hours a day for our church.

Lastly, I would like to thank the pastors and ministers of

my church. They are working together with me to raise as many faithful members as possible, praying continually and serving devotedly. They are working harder and harder to accomplish the missions God has given on behalf of me, where I can't go and work. I really appreciate their devotion and service.

My church family and I have hope for the heavenly kingdom. Now we don't see clearly the rewards we will receive in heaven. But we will keep marching toward the day when we receive great love from God in the beautiful kingdom of heaven, our original home land.

7

MY BELOVED ONE

All the glory to God

When we had the first overnight worship service in our new sanctuary, it was December 31, 1984. This New Year's Eve service ended in the early morning on January 1, 1985. All of the attendants were very happy to welcome the new year in the big new sanctuary. Due to rapid growth, our church had no more space for newcomers to sit. So God blessed us to move to a more spacious place. How wonderful His blessing is! For us to move into a new sanctuary was like the Israelites escaped from Egypt under the guiding hand of Moses, suffered in desert for 40 years, and finally went into the land of Canaan.

God led us to move into a new sanctuary

My church members were rapidly increasing. So we prayed for a place larger than 3,500 square feet. We found a place, which was pretty old but spacious. However, we couldn't sign the contract. The owner told us that he would tear the building down and construct a new one. We had to try to find a different place, but there was no building bigger than 3,500 square feet in Daebang-dong area.

We kept praying for the new sanctuary until we found a piece of land big enough for a temporary building. The landowner allowed us to start the construction for a temporary building. The local government personnel, however, came and pulled down the building we were constructing, because our construction was violating new regulations.

Because of this, a few members, although they trusted in me, complained. "God has led us with the pillar of cloud and the pillar of fire so far. Why does He let us construct an illegal building and leave it to be pulled down wastefully?"

I earnestly prayed to God. "Father, I know You cause all things to work together for the good. I thank You for Your special plan to lead us here at this point. I thank You for my congregation who also thanks You. Father, I have a few members who are complaining. Why have You left us in this suffering? Please let Your servant know clearly about Your plan, so that I can make all of my congregation understand it and thank You, believe in You and obey You. Please bless us to move into a larger building where we may guide more and more people to salvation, accomplishing the world mission too."

God listened to my earnest prayer, and He talked to me about His plan to lead us. I explained this plan to my congregation.

"Dear congregation, God said in Hebrews 11:1, *'Now faith is the assurance of things hoped for, the conviction of things not seen.' And He said in James 1:2-4, 'Consider it all joy, my brethren, when you encounter various trials, knowing that the testing of your faith produces endurance. And let endurance have its perfect result, so that you may be perfect and complete, lacking in nothing.'*

Did you rejoice when you faced trials? 1 Thessalonians 5:16-18 say, *'Rejoice always; pray without ceasing; in everything give thanks; for this is God's will for you in Christ Jesus.'* Have you lived by the will of God? Please understand that God allows us to face the testing of our faith to develop our perseverance completely.

The Israelites experienced many miraculous works of God, but they grumbled against God about their inconvenience in the wilderness. It is because they did not know and trust that God wanted to lead them to Canaan, a land flowing with milk and honey. How did we do? Aren't we like them?

I believe God will give us a great sanctuary just as He gave the Israelites the land of Canaan. Let's overcome this testing of our faith with perseverance, joy and thanks, so we may go into our land of Canaan!"

All the members endured the trials and obediently followed me as if they were going toward the land of Canaan. Unknowingly, the faith of many members including Chairman of the Construction Committee was growing during those months when they faced the testing of faith.

How then, did God prepare the land of Canaan for us? It was truly amazing. The first place God gave us was the land on which the landowner planned to construct a new building. That's why we could not rent or move in. But, a little while later, God had the owner construct a building there and He blessed us to move in. Hallelujah!

It took forty years for the Israelites to enter the land of Canaan, which they could have reached within three days. Likewise, we had to stay in the wilderness for a while until we moved into the place God had first given to us.

Our stay in the wilderness strengthened the faith of the leaders and other members so that they came to obey and trust in me receiving revelation from God who causes everything to work together for the good. They realized that God never fails to perform what He has said through me. Nothing could be more thankful than this.

The commemorative worship service for moving into the new sanctuary was really an impressive one, like a gorgeous festival in which we recognized the grace, love and power of God. The whole area of our new sanctuary was overflowing with our joy.

My dear servant!

I wanted to be the servant who is loved by God and pleasing to Him.

God gave us the victory over the persecution we received when starting our church. He sent us many souls to be saved.

He blessed us to clearly realize that we could move into a new sanctuary by His providence. He worked on my entire congregation so that they came to trust and obey me as their shepherd. He will extend His kingdom through our Manmin Joong-ang Church as the ark of salvation for many newcomers. He wants me to spread and teach the heavenly gospel, heal every kind of disease and sickness, and take up my cross for people just as Jesus did.

I firmly made up my mind. 'God has trust in me. So I must become the servant who pleases Him more and more each day.'

I like the verse, Proverbs 8:17 very much. *"I love those who love me; and those who diligently seek me will find me."*

I have loved God. I have tried with all my heart to live according to the word because those who love God keep what He commands. As a result, I have received abundant blessings and love from God.

I like the eleventh chapter of Hebrews. Especially, verse 6, which is my favorite. "And without faith it is impossible to please God, because anyone who comes to him must believe that he exists and that he rewards those who earnestly seek him."

I pray and give up everything to God, not relying on any person, because I believe that the almighty God exists. I have done my pastoral duty with all my strength, because I believe that God prepares heaven and He rewards those who practice His word.

I hope all of my congregation may love God and keep His

commandments so that He may love them. We must believe that God exists and that He rewards those who earnestly seek Him.

I wish that all of my congregation may pray continually, do their best to perform their assignments, and live with the hope of rewards in heaven.

All the glory to God

I give all the glory and thanks to God who has controlled everything for us.

If I have been recognized as a good pastor by God, it is because of my fruits - myself, completely reborn, as well as Manmin Central Church with its entire congregation that the Lord has brought together through me. I know how precious my congregation is.

God has loved me so much. I have taught my congregation how they can receive the love of God. They have obeyed my instructions with all their heart so that they are bearing beautiful and abundant fruits.

After we started our church, we had a very wonderful incident. My three daughters and a young adult member were dying from gas poisoning. But all of them revived right after I laid my hands on them in prayer. Seeing this, my church members came to believe in the word stated in Mark 9:23, *"All things are possible to him who believes."* Since then, a lot more members were healed and gave glory to God more than before.

On a Sunday evening, a deaconess and a taxi driver rushed to bring in a young girl to me. The deaconess told me that her 5-year-old daughter and she were on the way home after they finished the afternoon service. While they were crossing the road right in front of their apartment building, a taxi from the opposite direction ran into them and hit her daughter. It made the girl fly 7 to 8 meters in the air, fall down to the ground, and lose her consciousness. This accident shocked the deaconess, but she told the taxi driver, who was driving to the hospital, to go to Manmin Central Church located in Daebang-dong.

"Are you telling me to take this unconscious child to a church? She will die! I can't do that!"

"Don't worry. If she receives my pastor's prayer, she will regain her consciousness right away."

"…"

"Please hurry to Daebang-dong."

"It's not my fault if she dies. You must take the responsibility."

The taxi driver could not understand. He was forced by her to bring her daughter to me. The driver looked very frightened, but the deaconess was calming herself down with faith. I could see what a strong faith she had, so I prayed earnestly for her daughter.

"Father God! You raise the dead. And You said, 'Everything is possible for him who believes.' This time, please listen to Your servant, look at the faith of the deaconess, and save her young daughter. Please magnify Your name through this dying girl!"

As soon as I finished my fervent prayer for her, her body began to show vital signs and the warmth of life. I told the driver, who was still trembling for fear, not to worry any more. I told him to take the child to the hospital to make sure that she was okay.

We heard of the girl pretty soon. "She regained consciousness in the taxi on the way to the hospital. And the doctor at hospital said that her X-ray examination showed no problem in her at all." All of my congregation gave glory to God, and they gained the assurance that if we pray to God with faith, He may raise the dead.

In this manner, God has shown many miracles to my congregation through me, their shepherd, so that their faith has grown by seeing and hearing these miracles, and they have come to live according to the word. Hallelujah!

Through Manmin Prayer Center, God has healed a lot of people who were mentally or physically sick and has trained the attendants to pray for His kingdom and His righteousness day and night.

And mission groups were organized. All units of every group often gather to pray and evangelize to non-believers. They became one in love, guiding many people to salvation. I give all thanks and glory to God, who has raised my congregation to this day.

Let me mention in-church organizations and mission

groups.

Manmin Kindergarten and Children's Sunday School take care of young children and elementary school students. Students' Sunday School takes charge of evangelizing to high school students and unbelieving families. They study hard to glorify God in their position as students. College Mission members are doing their best to spread the gospel all over college campuses. Young Adults' Mission and Canaan Mission that is organized with unmarried college graduates, are working for workplace evangelization and world mission; developing their abilities and talents sufficient enough to guide people to salvation so that they may glorify God.

The distribution business and dining business workers organized the Light and Salt Mission. This mission is organized in most of the department stores and restaurants in Seoul. They are extending their mission to cover the whole nation now.

The members of Married Men's Mission and Married Women's Mission are fully accomplishing their duties at home and at work. They play important roles as pillars in His kingdom, serving the church with all their strength and leading the mission groups domestically and internationally. How blessed and thankful they are!

Additionally, I give the glory to God for the ministers of God who are taking good care of members with love. God is leading them to go out front for guiding many souls and for accomplishing the world mission.

'Father, You have led my congregation (children, students,

young adults, married men and women), pastors and ministers to become one in heart, to live by Your will, and to completely accomplish all the duties You have given them.

I give all thanks and glory to You! Please magnify Your name through Your children and Your servants day by day, all the time, until the Lord comes.'

By His will

I have served to follow after the will of God who cherishes a single soul as more precious than all the nations. I gave all thanks and glory to God who sent many souls to be saved and raised them to be faithful workers.

One day while I was receiving revelation from God, He talked to me about my rewards in heaven in great detail. I was astonished and embarrassed, because His rewards for me were far greater than anything I had done for Him. How should I thank Him for His love? I couldn't help crying out of pure gratitude.

Only by His will

God wanted me to follow only His will. He told me to put my hope in heaven and to save many souls so that I may reap heavenly rewards and glory to come, no matter how hard I might suffer from trials.

God was so kind and merciful. He let me hear of my appearance in heaven through my church members who had often received clear inspiration from God.

"Reverend, I saw you dwelling in heaven. You were with our church members, wearing a crown and special attire like a long robe. Your crown was beautifully glittering."

I knew what rewards I would receive in heaven, so I cautiously pledged myself to live a righteous life by the will of God.

"He who loves father or mother more than Me is not worthy of Me; and he who loves son or daughter more than Me is not worthy of Me. And he who does not take his cross and follow after Me is not worthy of Me. He who has found his life will lose it, and he who has lost his life for My sake will find it" (Matthew 10:37-39).

"Then Peter said to Him, 'Behold, we have left everything and followed You; what then will there be for us?' And Jesus said to them, 'Truly I say to you, that you who have followed Me, in the regeneration when the Son of Man will sit on His glorious throne, you also shall sit upon twelve thrones, judging the twelve tribes of Israel. And everyone who has left houses or brothers or sisters or father or mother or children or farms for My name's sake, will receive many times as much, and will inherit eternal life'" (Matthew 19:27-29).

"For whoever does the will of My Father who is in heaven, he is My brother and sister and mother"

(Matthew 12:50).

God wants us to love Him, live by His will and glorify Him by guiding many souls to salvation, so that we may receive His rewards in heaven. Because He bought us with Jesus' blood on the cross, we ought to live our lives by the will of God as His children, returning the grace we received.

Then, what is the will of God? Just as man scatters seeds in the fields to harvest crops in fall, God planted mankind in this world. With God a day is like a thousand years, and a thousand years is like a day. As He created all creatures in the universe for six days and rested on the seventh day, He cultivates mankind in this world for 6,000 years and lets believers rest in His kingdom for 1,000 years. And by the Last Judgment He will separate the wheat from the chaff, that is, He will gather the righteous into heaven, who will shine like the sun, and throw the wicked into the fiery furnace.

Why does God cultivate mankind for 6,000 years? Since God created man, he obeyed Him and lived countless long years in the Garden of Eden. Adam and Eve, however, disobeyed God and were thrown out of the Garden of Eden. Since then, their spirit died, so they became men of flesh, living by their own will not by the will of God.

For the next 2,000 years God saw how great man's wickedness on the earth had become, and that every inclination of the thoughts of his heart was only evil all the time. So God destroyed all of mankind except for Noah and his family, for Noah was a righteous man, blameless among the people of his time. After Noah, Abraham was born and eventually the twelve sons of Jacob established Israel. God raised the Israelites for another 2,000 years letting them know His will through prophets. He disciplined the Israelites to know that He is the lawgiver and the judge, reigning over all of them.

By God's providence Jesus came to us so that we can be justified by faith. 2,000 years of human history has passed since Jesus came to this earth. It is written in the Bible, *"This Jesus, who has been taken up from you into heaven, will come in just the same way as you have watched Him go into heaven"* (Acts 1:11). We must prepare ourselves for the Second Advent of Christ.

God has both human attributes and divine attributes. He wants us to be His true children who may exchange love with Him. We must keep in mind that God has waited for thousands of years to gain the grain, His true children.

How can we be the true children?

What should we do to be His true children who live by His will?

First, we must throw away our wickedness and live holy lives to be men of spirit.

If we accept Jesus Christ, we are made right by believing in our heart and are saved by confessing with our mouth. So our spirit desires to live by the will of God as the Spirit wants, not to live for fleshly lust as the sinful nature wants.

If we hear and read the word, the Spirit helps us live by the will of God as the Spirit wants. Thus we become men of spirit who live holy lives. Men of spirit always rejoice, pray continually, and give thanks in all circumstances.

Secondly, we must work hard and accomplish our duties to receive our rewards in heaven.

God is extending His kingdom through us, His workers. We have to accomplish our own duties as family members, as students, as employees, and as church members. We must complete all those duties to receive our full reward in heaven.

Thirdly, we must please and glorify God.

God wants to receive glory through us. God wants us to serve the community as light and salt so that others may come to believe in God through our characters. He also wants us to be a kernel of wheat that falls to the ground and dies but produces many seeds. He wants us to enjoy good health. And He wants that all may go well with us, even as our soul is getting along well, so that we may glorify God.

Forsaking my thoughts

If you want to live by the will of God, you have to forsake your thoughts derived from your sinful nature first. You might wonder how you can get rid of fleshly thoughts, but it is easy.

I have lived my life according only to the word of God, the truth. Jesus lived like that, and so did Paul the apostle. If you believe in God, you can easily live by the truth.

How can we forsake our fleshly thoughts?

If we demolish arguments and every pretension that sets itself up against the knowledge of God, and we take captive every thought to make it obedient to Christ, our fleshly thoughts disappear so that we come to obey just as the Holy Spirit desires. In other words, although you are wise, educated, and experienced, if you find anything in you against the truth, you must forsake it. Then you can go as the truth leads you. If you arm yourself with the truth and practice what it says, you come to hear the voice of the Holy Spirit clearly. Although you may encounter unexpected incidents, you will not try to solve them with your own knowledge or thoughts, but you will solve them as the Holy Spirit speaks to your heart.

Jesus followed God's will that He must die on the cross. He was absolutely innocent, but He was crucified only by God's will.

"And He was saying, Abba! Father! All things are possible for You; remove this cup from Me; yet not what I will, but what You will" (Mark 14:36).

Paul the apostle, five times he received from the Jews the forty lashes minus one. Three times he was beaten with rods, once he was stoned, three times he was shipwrecked, he spent a night and a day in the open sea, and he was in danger several times during his ministerial journeys. He knew that God selected him to accomplish His will, spreading the gospel to Gentiles, their kings, and descendants of the Israelites.

Our present sufferings are not worth comparing with the glory that will be revealed in us

God has prepared the glory for Jesus Christ to sit at His right hand, and for Paul the apostle, to receive the crown of righteousness and rewards in heaven.

God encouraged me by revealing what rewards I will be given in heaven. I have hope for the heavenly kingdom, so I have thrown away every kind of evil to live a holy life, accomplishing the world mission and getting myself totally armed with the word. I am going to do miraculous signs and wonders wherever I go, crossing over the mountains, the hills, and the seas, to guide the dying souls to salvation, to change the chaff into the wheat, and to give all the glory to God.

We must not be those who only call, 'Lord, Lord!' but also be those who accomplish the will of God, so that we may enter the everlasting beautiful kingdom of heaven. I hope that my congregation throw away every kind of evil to live a holy life, accomplishing all good works to glorify God.

I wanted to live like Jesus. So I forsook my own will to keep the word, and I did not love my wife, my children, or my belongings better than God. Because of this, God called me as His servant who would accomplish the world mission and get blessed with great rewards in heaven.

I feel very happy that I, as the shepherd guiding a large number of flocks, will complete all of my assignments and enter the everlasting kingdom of heaven.

Everlasting life in heaven

As John the apostle had communed with God on the island of Patmos, I used to be in an isolated place to receive revelation from God.

A clean river was flowing peacefully in front of the house where I was staying. A thickly wooded mountain was behind the house. Various crops were growing in the wide-open field. That area was so unfrequented that the natural beauty was well preserved. When I crossed the river by boat, the breeze touched me refreshingly, and the birds were joyfully flying in the blue sky as if they were greeting me. The soil was very soft like fine sand, and the pebbles rolling along the riverside were pretty.

God had me stay there for a while reading the Bible and praying. It was very far from Seoul, so I had to spend many hours to get there. But it was worthwhile. There I enjoyed the freshness I could not feel in Seoul, and it sometimes made me imagine heaven.

God revealed to me the heavenly kingdom

It was in May 1984, a few days before my birthday. I usually came down from the mountain on Friday to prepare for Friday overnight service and Sunday services. However, God told me not to go down but to fast because He would tell me about the heavenly kingdom.

Suddenly the gate of heaven opened in front of my eyes and God began to speak to me. He revealed many things to me for the whole week from Monday. I was happy beyond words. I gave all thanks and glory to God for His love.

I believe God wanted me to know that to receive the gift from God through fasting and praying was a lot better for His kingdom and myself than to get earthly pleasure out of my birthday party.

He told me many parables of heaven:

'The kingdom of heaven is like a man who sows good seed in his field.' 'The kingdom of heaven is like a net that is let down into the lake to catch all kinds of fish.' This parable means that angels come at the end of the world to lead the righteous to heaven and throw the wicked into the fiery furnace of hell.

There is not a righteous man on earth. So we must believe in Jesus Christ, who is the way and the truth and the life, to be justified and to enter and live in heaven. In heaven there is everlasting joy and peace. On the contrary, those who do not believe in Jesus Christ are wicked, so they are thrown into eternal punishment in hell. In hell the worms do not die, and the fire is not quenched.

The Judgment of the Great White Throne will separate the believers from non-believers: the believers into eternal life, but the non-believers into eternal punishment. This is the end of 7,000 years of history, including 6,000 years of the cultivation of man on the earth and 1,000 years of living on the renewed earth. Then the eternal life comes after.

Many places to live in the heavenly kingdom

"Do not let your heart be troubled; believe in God, believe also in Me. In My Father's house are many dwelling places; if it were not so, I would have told you; for I go to prepare a place for you. If I go and prepare a place for you, I will come again and receive you to Myself, that where I am, there you may be also" (John 14:1-3).

We understand that we were born not by our own will but by the will of someone else. He is God. We must consider that God determines where each of us stays eternally according to how we have followed His will.

God is just. He lets us reap what we sow. If we sow faith, He lets us reap heaven. If we do not sow faith, He lets us reap hell. And He gives us the dwelling places and the rewards in heaven according to how obediently we have lived by His will. He does not reward everyone equally with the same thing.

In the Bible we read that there are many rooms in heaven. 2 Corinthians 12:2 says about 'the third heaven.' Deuteronomy 10:14 talks about 'the heavens, even the highest heavens.' Psalm 148:4 talks about 'the highest heavens.' 1 Kings 8:27 and Nehemiah 9:6 tell us about 'the heavens, even the highest heavens.' The Bible repeatedly mentions different aspects of heaven that there are many levels in heaven, more than just one in our Father's house.

God spoke to me through the Holy Spirit while I was reading the Bible with the hope that I might clearly understand His will on 'the heavens.' From now I will describe the heavens based on the revelation God has given me: Paradise, the First Kingdom, the Second Kingdom, the Third Kingdom and New Jerusalem.

Romans 12:3 says, *"For through the grace given to me I say to everyone among you not to think more highly of himself than he ought to think; but to think so as to have sound judgment, as God has allotted to each a measure of faith."* If there were no difference in the measure of faith, no one would exert himself (herself) to have a greater measure of faith. It is easy to find that the measure of faith is critical.

On the one hand, Jesus rebuked His disciples in Mark 4:40, *"Why are you afraid? How is it that you have no faith?"* On the other hand, He praised a Roman centurion for his great faith in Matthew 8:10, *"Truly I say to you, I have not found such great faith with anyone in Israel."* I came to understand that everyone differs in his own measure of faith, and so, the place in which each one dwells in heaven is determined in accordance with his measure of faith.

Let me describe these places and the rewards given in heaven, in accordance with the measure of faith from the smallest to the greatest.

The crucified criminal, who repented of his sins as Jesus was being crucified, merely accepted Jesus Christ. He had not struggled with sin and he had not lived according to the word. He had no deeds to show his faith as evidence of practicing the word, but only repented and accepted Jesus Christ. So he was given Paradise to live in.

The next step of faith is of those who try to live according to the word they hear, but cannot practice all that they hear. The First Kingdom is given for them to live in. They will receive a crown that lasts forever because they have struggled to cast away their sins (1 Corinthians 9:25).

The next step of faith is of those who live by the word, fighting against their sins and glorifying God. The Second Kingdom is given to them. And they will receive the crown of glory that will never fade away because they have thrown away their sins (1 Peter 5:4).

The next step of faith is of those who live completely by the word and love God with their heart. The Third Kingdom is given to them. They will receive the crown of life because they have been faithful even to the point of death (James 1:12; Revelation 2:10).

The highest level of faith is of those who love God with all their heart so that they please Him. New Jerusalem is given to them. They will receive the crown of righteousness (2 Timothy 4:8) or the crown of gold (Revelation 4:4) because they have become holy and completed all their works assigned to them.

Likewise, God gives us a place to live and the reward in heaven in accordance with our measure of faith. So we must work hard, living a holy life according to His will, to advance to the better heavenly kingdom.

The differences between heavens are very significant. Here in Korea, we can tell the difference in living conditions among the capital city Seoul, other provincial cities, country between the capital city Seoul and other provincial cities, countryside towns and islands. We know why so many people want to come to Seoul. By the same token, we are trying to advance to New Jerusalem, because we know that the places in heaven differ.

Let's say a man who resides in New Jerusalem is visiting the Second Kingdom. The people in the Second Kingdom cannot look at him who came from New Jerusalem because his light glows too brightly for them. So they kneel down to show their respect like the common people do when their king passes. The glories of each heaven are completely different. Oppositely, the people in the Second Kingdom cannot enter New Jerusalem because their light is different from that of the people in New Jerusalem and because the angels are guarding at the gates.

Now you know about the eternal life in heaven. What kingdom do you want to live in? It will be determined by how much you have obeyed the will of God.

Houses also differ by the kingdom of heaven you live in. In Paradise no individual house is given because they have not practiced the word in their lifetime. On the contrary, the houses are constructed almost completely out of gold and precious stones for the believers who have obeyed the word with deeds.

Heaven belongs to the world we call 'the fourth dimension,' rising above time and space. We can imagine that in many ways the features of earth resemble those of heaven. In this fourth dimensional world, we can fly as we want. Everyone who lives in heaven has the new spiritual body that never perishes and seems to have no weight. Life in heaven is so wonderful and everlasting.

What does heaven look like?

The river of the water of life flows from the throne of God, passes around the Third Kingdom, the Second Kingdom, the First Kingdom and Paradise, and returns to the throne of God.

Can you imagine how beautiful it will be to walk along the river of the pure water of life, as clear as crystal? Along the riversides are banks spread over with brightly glittering sands of gold and silver. The taste of the water of life is too pure and fresh to be compared with any water on the earth.

In heaven, things are made of precious stones and pure gold. There is no dirt or dust, and no thief can break in. The roads are made of gold, and we can see all kinds of God's creature. Can you imagine how beautiful?

All kinds of plants and animals are in proper arrangement. There are special flower passages. You can talk with animals and flowers or sit on them while you are walking.

The trees of life bear twelve kinds of fruits. Every fruit tastes different and looks different from each other. If you pick any fruit from any tree, the tree instantly produces the same kind of fruit in the same place. How awesome this is!

When you eat, you may physically eat with your mouth or you may enjoy the smells of food. After you have food, you feel satisfied and filled with strength. How do you suppose they digest and eliminate? Of course there are no dirty bathrooms in heaven. After they eat food, they digest inside their body and they eliminate it as fragrant gas while they breathe. The fragrance stays in the air for a while and disappears. How convenient is that?

What do we look like in heaven?

We look like the image of resurrected Jesus. We have spirit, soul and imperishable body - imperishable bones and flesh. With our heavenly bodies we can pass through walls, so we do not have to open any doors.

Our physical features will be like those of Jesus at the age of 33. Our faces will be shiny like a white gem. Our height will be about 180 cm for men, and women are a little shorter. The hair of every man is as long as to reach the neck. The length of women's hair varies according to their own rewards. The greater her rewards are, the longer her hair is. Some women have the hair reaching their hip. You do not have to worry about the defects of your present body. In heaven your bodies have the best features. What a happy thing this is!

You will not be married to each other in heaven. As spiritual bodies, you recognize your family - your spouse, children and parents. You recognize your shepherd and your flock. You can live with your earthly family and you can gather with your church members. Your spirit is very wise, so your wisdom will be a hundred times what you have on earth.

What is the living in heaven like?

God gives us clothes made of fine linen, and He rewards us many precious ornaments according to what we have done. That is because God wants us to wear those precious ornaments to show His love and glory. He also lets us ride on His clouds of glory. We often gather at the feasts, having a pleasant time and conversation together, and watching the video films that present our earthly lives. There will be a lot more wonderful and marvelous things in heaven.

God revealed to me the hidden things of heaven, but I cannot let you know all of them for now. Lately I have published two books on heaven.

We know this wonderful heaven exists. That is why we are looking forward to the day when the Lord who has prepared these places in heaven for us comes again, and we are living by the will of God.

In this world also, if you work hard, you can go to good schools, get good jobs, take supervisory positions, and good houses. In the same way, you will be given the place, the crown, and the reward in accordance with how faithfully you lived on earth. Those things in heaven are given to you eternally. This is why everyone wants to receive as much of these beautiful things as possible.

Jesus spoke about the independence of Israel with the parable of a fig tree, *"Now learn the parable from the fig tree: when its branch has already become tender and puts forth its leaves, you know that summer is near;*

So, you too, when you see all these things, recognize that He is near, right at the door. Truly I say to you, this generation will not pass away until all these things take place" (Matthew 24:32-34).

"Therefore be on the alert, for you do not know which day your Lord is coming.But be sure of this, that if the head of the house had known at what time of the night the thief was coming, he would have been on the alert and would not have allowed his house to be broken into" (Matthew 24:42-43).

"While they are saying, 'Peace and safety!' then destruction will come upon them suddenly like labor pains upon a woman with child, and they will not escape. But you, brethren, are not in darkness, that the day would overtake you like a thief; for you are all sons of light and sons of day. We are not of night nor of darkness; so then let us not sleep as others do, but let us be alert and sober" (1 Thessalonians 5:3-6).

God told us that the Second Coming is very near. No one knows about that day and hour. God told me as well as some faithful believers who are awake that the last hour is very near. How many people will know they will be lifted up alive in the air?

It makes me very happy to think of the days to come when we will live with the Lord in His everlasting world.

I am working hard today to accomplish my duties and feed

my flock in a good pasture.

"Amen, Come, Lord Jesus!"

The Author
Dr. Jaerock Lee

Dr. Jaerock Lee was born in Muan, Jeonnam Province, Republic of Korea, in 1943. In his twenties, he suffered from a variety of incurable diseases for seven years and awaited death with no hope for recovery. One day in the spring of 1974, however, he was led to a church by his sister, and when he knelt down to pray, the living God immediately healed him of all his diseases.

From the moment Dr. Lee met the living God through that wonderful experience, he has loved God with all his heart and sincerity, and in 1978 was called to be a servant of God. He prayed fervently so that he could clearly understand the will of God and wholly accomplish it, and obeyed all the word of God. In 1982, he founded Manmin Church in Seoul, S. Korea, and countless works of God, including miraculous healings and wonders, have been taking place at his church.

In 1986, Dr. Lee was ordained as a pastor at the Annual Assembly of Jesus' Sungkyul Church of Korea, and four years later in 1990, his sermons began to be broadcast on the Far East Broadcasting Company, the Asia Broadcast Station, and the Washington Christian Radio System to Australia, Russia, the Philippines, and many more.

Three years later in 1993, Manmin Central Church was selected as one of the "World's Top 50 Churches" by the *Christian World* magazine (US) and he received an Honorary Doctorate of Divinity from Christian Faith College, Florida, USA, and in 1996 a Ph. D. in Ministry from Kingsway Theological Seminary, Iowa, USA.

Since 1993, Dr. Lee has taken the lead in world mission through many overseas crusades in L.A., New York, Baltimore, Hawaii of the USA, Tanzania, Argentina, Uganda, Japan, Pakistan, Kenya, the Philippines,

Honduras, India, Russia, Germany, Peru, and Democratic Republic of Congo, and in 2002 he was called a "worldwide pastor" by major Christian newspapers in Korea for his work in various overseas crusades.

As of August 2009, Manmin Central Church is a congregation of more than 100,000 members and has 9,000 branch churches throughout the globe including 52 domestic branch churches in major cities, and has so far commissioned more than 132 missionaries to 25 countries, including the United States, Russia, Germany, Canada, Japan, China, France, India, Kenya, and many more.

To this day, Dr. Lee has written 57 books, including bestsellers *Tasting Eternal Life before Death, My Life My Faith I & II, The Way of Salvation, The Measure of Faith, Heaven I & II,* and *Hell,* and his works have been being translated into more than 41 languages.

His Christian columns appear on *The Hankook Ilbo, The JoongAng Daily, The Dong-A Ilbo, The Munhwa Ilbo, The Seoul Shinmun, The Kyunghyang Shinmun, The Hankyoreh Shinmun, The Korea Economic Daily, The Korea Herald, The Shisa News, The Christian Press* and *The Nation Evangelization Newspaper.*

Dr. Lee is currently leader of many missionary organizations and associations including: Chairman, The United Holiness Church of Jesus Christ; Permanent President of the World Christianity Revival Mission Association; President, The Nation Evangelization Newspaper; President, Manmin World Mission; Founder, Manmin TV; Founder & Board Chairman, Global Christian Network (GCN); Founder & Board Chairman, World Christian Doctors Network (WCDN); and Founder & Board Chairman, Manmin International Seminary (MIS).

Heaven I & II

A detailed sketch of the gorgeous living environment the heavenly citizens enjoy and beautiful description of different levels of heavenly kingdoms.

The Message of the Cross

A powerful awakening message for all the people who are spiritually asleep In this book you will find the reason Jesus is the only Savior and the true love of God.

Hell

An earnest message to all mankind from God, who wishes not even one soul to fall into the depths of hell! You will discover the never-before-revealed account of the cruel reality of the Lower Grave and hell.

The Measure of Faith

What kind of a dwelling place, crown and reward are prepared for you in heaven? This book provides with wisdom and guidance for you to measure your faith and cultivate the best and most mature faith.

Awaken Israel

Why has God kept His eyes on Israel from the beginning of the world to this day? What kind of His providence has been prepared for Israel in the last days, who await the Messiah?